Blue Lacy

A Blue Lacy Dog Owner's Guide

Blue Lacy Basics, Choosing and Owning, Breeding, Care, Nutrition, Grooming, Showing and Training All Included!

By: Lolly Brown

Copyrights and Trademarks

All rights reserved. No part of this book may be reproduced or transformed in any form or by any means, graphic, electronic, or mechanical, including photocopying, recording, taping, or by any information storage retrieval system, without the written permission of the author.

This publication is Copyright ©2021 NRB Publishing, an imprint of Pack & Post Plus, LLC. Nevada. All products, graphics, publications, software and services mentioned and recommended in this publication are protected by trademarks. In such instance, all trademarks & copyright belong to the respective owners. For information consult www.NRBpublishing.com

Disclaimer and Legal Notice

This product is not legal, medical, or accounting advice and should not be interpreted in that manner. You need to do your own due-diligence to determine if the content of this product is right for you. While every attempt has been made to verify the information shared in this publication, neither the author, neither publisher, nor the affiliates assume any responsibility for errors, omissions or contrary interpretation of the subject matter herein. Any perceived slights to any specific person(s) or organization(s) are purely unintentional.

We have no control over the nature, content and availability of the web sites listed in this book. The inclusion of any web site links does not necessarily imply a recommendation or endorse the views expressed within them. We take no responsibility for, and will not be liable for, the websites being temporarily unavailable or being removed from the internet.

The accuracy and completeness of information provided herein and opinions stated herein are not guaranteed or warranted to produce any particular results, and the advice and strategies, contained herein may not be suitable for every individual. Neither the author nor the publisher shall be liable for any loss incurred as a consequence of the use and application, directly or indirectly, of any information presented in this work. This publication is designed to provide information in regard to the subject matter covered.

Neither the author nor the publisher assume any responsibility for any errors or omissions, nor do they represent or warrant that the ideas, information, actions, plans, suggestions contained in this book is in all cases accurate. It is the reader's responsibility to find advice before putting anything written in this book into practice. The information in this book is not intended to serve as legal, medical, or accounting advice.

Foreword

The instructional guide will discuss all of the things that you need to know in order to get started with raising training your new Blue Lacy puppy. Bringing home a new addition for the first time can be a really exciting endeavor. The whole family may have spent time picking out the puppy that they wanted to bring home, and now they are excited to bond with her and to make some lasting memories.

This guidebook is going to walk you through the steps that you need to follow in order to raise your Blue Lacy well, get your puppy trained and ready to behave.

Included inside this book's first section is about the origin and bio of a Blue Lacy. It also contains information about its breed appearance, personality temperament and behavior.

The Second section is about choosing a Blue Lacy. It tackles about where and how to acquire a Blue Lacy and how to select a healthy Blue Lacy puppy.

The next section will talk about the things that you need and have to do as a Blue Lacy owner.

The fourth section focuses on how you can cater your dog's nutritional needs.

The fifth section is about raising and training your Blue Lacy. It educates dog owners about the importance of training and activities for your dog. It additionally contains a puppy's training outline and guidance in shaping behaviors, training, and problem solving.

The next section delves into basic care and regular grooming needs for your Blue Lacy.

Th seventh section focuses on the common health issues and how to deal with them and respond into emergencies.

Chapter eight is about preparing your Blue Lacy for a dog show.

For the last section, it will talk about the breeding process for your Blue Lacy.

By obtaining this training guide, you will be on your way to securing the necessary tools and knowledge to assure your success as a dog owner and trainer.

Table of Contents

Introduction 1

Chapter One: Blue Lacy Origin 3

    History 3

    Physical Characteristics 5

    Blue Lacy Personality & Characteristics 6

    Temperament and Behavior 6

Chapter Two: Choosing a Blue Lacy 7

    The Right Time for a Puppy 7

    Where to Get Your Puppy 8

        Shelters 8

        Rescues 9

        Breeders 10

        Other Places 11

    Checking the Health Status 12

Chapter Three: Owning a Blue Lacy 13

    Supplies Needed 13

        Living Supplies 14

        Dietary Supplies 16

        Cleaning Supplies 18

        Grooming Supplies 20

Training Supplies 22

Miscellaneous Supplies 23

Puppy-proofing Your Home 25

Dealing with Separation Anxiety 30

Chapter Four: Nutrition for Blue Lacy 33

What to Feed Your Puppy 33

Dry Kibble 34

Wet Food 35

Raw Food 35

Special Diets 36

Water 37

Supplements 38

List of Approved Foods and their Nutrients 39

List of Toxic Foods for Blue Lacy 43

Chapter Five: Raising and Training a Blue Lacy 47

The Top Commands to Teach Your Blue Lacy Puppy 47

Sit 48

Lay Down 49

Stay 51

Wait 52

Come 54

Leave It 56

    Touch 58

    Shake 59

    Heel 61

Correcting Behavior Problems 64

    Shushing the Barker 65

    Barking for Attention 65

    Barking at Everything 66

    Not Accepting Biting 69

    Getting Chewing Under Control 70

    Stopping the Digging Frenzy 72

    Discouraging the Jumper 74

    Turning Away from the Jump 75

    Use Commands 75

    Go Out the Door 75

House Training 76

    Observe the Signs 76

    Some Basic Rules to Follow 77

    Routine is a Must 78

    Little Things to Keep in Mind 79

    Dealing with Accidents 80

    Crate Training 81

    Combine toilet training with sleep training 81

>> Just Keep Going 82

Training Your Dog for Public Situations 82

>> How to Walk Your Dog 83

>> Using Obedience Training During Walks 87

Chapter Six: Grooming Your Blue Lacy 91

Grooming and Parasites 91

Tools and Methods 93

Bathing your Blue Lacy 95

Trimming your dog's nails 98

Cleaning your dog's ears 99

Brushing your Blue Lacy's teeth 100

Chapter Seven: Vet Care for Your Blue Lacy 103

Common Illnesses and Injuries 103

>> What's Normal? 104

>> When should blood work be done? 105

>> The Annual Exam 105

>> Problem Visits 105

Relieving Blue Lacy Allergies 106

>> Inhalant Allergies 106

>> Food Allergies 107

>> Diagnosing Allergies 108

>> Cuts and Scrapes 109

Dealing with Foxtails 109

Relief from Hot Spots 110

Lumps and Bumps 110

Gastrointestinal Problems 111

Lack of Appetite 113

Ear Infections 113

Treating Ear Infections 113

Lameness or Limping 115

Chapter Eight: Showing Your Blue Lacy 117

How Do You Know If Your Dog Is Good Enough to Show? 118

Preparing to Show Your Dog 119

What Age Does My Dog Need to Be to Start to Show? .. 119

Training for the Show Ring 122

What to take 124

Chapter Nine: Breeding Your Blue Lacy 127

Basic Breeding Information 128

The Breeding Process 130

The stud dog 132

Stages of Pregnancy 132

Maintaining everyday care 133

Raising Blue Lacy Puppies 134

Conclusion 143
   Glossary of Dog Terms.. 145
Photo Credits 159
References 161

Introduction

Dogs are taken as great partners for families across the globe. However, if you desire for a well-behaved dog that perfectly fits in with your friends and family, then you need to master some dog training basics. There will be multiple forms of training that you can discover in the chapters ahead, a few more substantial and famous than the others, you can pick one that heeds you comfortable and you will also be taught wonderful tricks to procure the best results in a short span of time. Keep in mind that your pet dog is now like your family member who will need the same attention, care, and love like any other member of your family. I will discuss a few invaluable methods, using which, you can easily earn your dog's love and trust and teach him to look after himself efficiently. This book will help you teach your dog to behave smartly and in a gentle manner, also making him act independently. Or simply, you will be able to train your canine matching your own specifications, in such a manner that it would not result in any fatigue or trouble for both you and your pet.

Once you have made up your mind to adopt a pet, then getting some basic things for him is not an arduous task, but the major problem arises when you realize that your pup would need some training too. Knowing from where to begin your journey of training a dog is occasionally the hardest thing. You will want to begin from the basics and work from there.

Training will strengthen the relationship with your dog, and over passing years the developed bond will deepen.

Introduction

It will become a lot easier to get along with and fully comprehend each other's need and limitations once you master the skills needed to communicate with each other.

Trust me, providing your dog with some basic training is the most loving thing that you could do towards him and if he had the ability to speak, he would be thanking you all his life. Training your dog guarantees that he is safe and welcome everywhere he moves and that he is comfortable to live with. This book will open the key to every secret kept hidden to you until now in this regard and will guarantee you a smooth and unhalted process. I am profoundly gratified towards you for confiding in me and allowing me to be of a little aid in helping your pooch.

Let's get started!

Chapter One: Blue Lacy Origin

History

The Blue Lacy has numerous nicknames including the the Lacy Hog Dog, Lacy Cur, or merely the Lacy dog. This dog gets its designation from the first family who bred them. Four siblings: Frank, Harry, Ewin, and George Lacy are known to have moved from Kentucky to Burnet, Texas in 1858.

Chapter One: Blue Lacy Origin

In the same way as other different breeders at that time, they kept 'cur' or mixed breed canines to offer insurance, and to fill in as herders and hunters. The Lacy family were cognizant in the reproducing of their homestead canines, and over the long run built up the Blue Lacy.

The combination of breeds used to build up the Blue Lacy is exceptionally discussed, however is thought to incorporate the Greyhound, the English Shepherd, and a scent-hound. It is proclaimed that a wild creature, for example, a wolf or coyote, likewise added to the blend of canines used.

The Blue Lacy soon gained a nice standing in Texas and was valued by numerous individuals for its herding and hunting capacities. While they were generally used to work with domestic pigs, they are known to be entirely versatile and are really used to work with all types of animals and chase a scope of prey, including raccoons, wild boar, and squirrels.

While they were sought after on family farms constantly in the Southern United States for a long time, with the arrival of ranch vehicles and the diminishing fame of smallholder farming, there was a time when the Blue Lacy was near eradication. Fortunately, their verifiable working abilities and amazing pace guaranteed that their prominence was soon restored. It is a canine of numerous talents and have

Chapter One: Blue Lacy Origin

a variety uses ranging from the more traditional hunting, treeing, blood-trailing and tracking, to competing in modern-day obedience, agility, and flyball.

They are, indeed, the most regularly utilized breed in the game of 'trapping' today. This is a disputable strategy for ' trapping nuisance creatures, for example, foxes and raccoons in man-made traps. The Blue Lacy will make the rancher or the hunter aware of the presence of the prey by yelping.

Regardless of their general fame, it wasn't until 2001 that the Texas Senate perceived the Blue Lacy as its own variety of dog. Shortly after, in June 2005, it was authoritatively proclaimed 'The State Dog of Texas'; a remarkable award. While their prominence is ever expanding in the United States, they are generally unfamiliar in the present reality, with only little numbers in Europe.

Physical Characteristics

The Blue Lacy is a medium pure breed pet canine that comes from the herding group. Male Blue Lacy canines usually show up at 30-50 pounds (13-23 kg) and 18-23 inches (46-58 cm) while women reach in 30-50 pounds (13-23 kg) and 18-23 inches (46-58 cm). Regarding their looks, Blue Lacys is regularly toned Blue, Cream, Dark Gray, Red, Silver, or Tricolor. Their external coat has immaterial sheddings and they are low maintenance canines not needing fancy grooming.

Blue Lacy Personality & Characteristics

Blue Lacys belongs to Herding dog group and has the following characteristics:

- Alert
- Devoted
- Bold
- Intense
- Intelligent

Temperament and Behavior

Dog types that come from the herding group are intelligent and energetic. Since they're territorial of "their" home and people, they make for terrific guard dogs. These dogs are really athletic have an urge for working. Herding dogs are smart and may be the most easy and convenient kind of pet to train. They are well suited for pet dog sports and competitions.

Herding pet dogs are suitable for large households; they like hanging out with groups of people. Even if you do not have a huge family but live on an expansive home with various animals, a herding dog will suit in.

Chapter Two: Choosing a Blue Lacy

The Right Time for a Puppy

So, you're thinking about adding a Blue Lacy to your family, but you're unsure when to do it. A pet will impact major areas of your life, like your schedule and finances, so there are a few considerations to keep in mind. First, a stable work schedule is important so you can plan your puppy's feeding and bathroom routine around your work hours. Does your job give you the flexibility needed to let your puppy outside during the day to go to the bathroom, or will you need to hire a dog walker or pet sitter to assist with this? Does your schedule allow additional time to devote to your puppy's

Chapter Two: Choosing a Blue Lacy

exercise and social needs? Blue Lacy puppies require a lot of time, attention, and guidance, especially in the early months, so you must be willing to prioritize them daily. Having funds set aside for regular feeding, grooming, and health care is also important, as are emergency funds for potential accidents or illnesses.

Where to Get Your Puppy

Where do puppies come from? There are several ways you can go about obtaining a puppy, and it's important to understand the pros and cons of each option.

Shelters

An animal shelter is a place that accepts lost, abandoned, or surrendered animals and provides health care and lodging with the goal of eventually finding them homes. An animal shelter might be your local pound or a nonprofit organization such as the Society for the Prevention of Cruelty to Animals (SPCA). When you adopt a puppy from a shelter, you're saving the lives of two animals: the one you're adopting and the next dog to occupy the kennel space you're freeing up. Shelter adoption fees generally include your puppy's vaccinations, deworming, spay or neuter surgery, and a form of permanent ID such as a tattoo or microchip. Adoption fees are generally much lower than a purchase fee from a registered dog breeder, which makes shelter puppies a more financially feasible option.

Chapter Two: Choosing a Blue Lacy

Shelters are preferable to other options in many ways, but finding a puppy at a shelter might be more difficult, as they're generally in higher demand than adult or senior dogs. The same goes for finding a purebred; most shelters have mixed-breed dogs and/or unclear information on the breeding of their dogs. Also, keep in mind that these animals might have been removed from abusive or negligent living situations, and a traumatic history can impact any animal's social development and behavior.

Rescues

Rescues differ from shelters in that they're privately owned facilities that deal with animals who have been surrendered by their owners or transferred there from animal shelters. Rescues typically place the animals in their care in foster homes, as opposed to the group environment of shelters. Being raised in a home helps the animals become accustomed to this type of lifestyle and provides them with regular social opportunities. Foster homes also tend to have more insight into the personality of the specific puppy you're looking to adopt, which can be helpful when trying to find the right match for you. In addition, rescues can be breed- and age-specific with the animals they care for, which is useful if you have a particular breed of puppy in mind. A rescue might have a more intensive application and interview process than a shelter, which helps ensure you and your chosen puppy are a great match—but it can also be tedious and time-consuming.

Chapter Two: Choosing a Blue Lacy

When adopting a Blue Lacy from either a shelter or a rescue, it's important to ask how or why they arrived at the facility. Knowing an animal's history can help you identify areas in which they may require more support when developing. A puppy who was rescued from a puppy mill will likely lack early exposure and socialization opportunities, and they may appear fearful. A puppy who has suffered abuse could have fears associated with specific noises, places, or types and appearances of people. These puppies will require patience and more proactive socialization than the average pup, so be sure that you're willing and able to take on this challenge.

Breeders

Choosing to go with a purebred puppy means you can research and select a breed that matches some of the qualities you want in your dog. When getting your Blue Lacy from a reputable breeder, you can often meet your puppy's parents, which can provide further insight into the temperament of your puppy as it matures, and you can see the environment in which your puppy was raised, which directly impacts its social development during the early weeks.

Breeding is an unregulated practice, and any person can identify themselves as a breeder, so it's critical to do your research. A reputable dog breeder invests a lot of time in caring for their dogs and finding them the right homes. They're likely devoting time and money to achieving titles at dog shows, and they are typically involved with their breed

Chapter Two: Choosing a Blue Lacy

club (an association of those who fancy a particular breed of dog, organized under a national kennel club, which decides on breed standards and showing regulations). A reputable breeder should be performing genetic and health testing and should provide you with the results of this testing when you purchase a puppy from them.

Purchasing a Blue Lacy from a breeder comes with a considerable price tag compared to a shelter's adoption fees, so it's important to budget for that. Remember to ask the breeder what vaccines and deworming the puppy has had, as each breeder will have their own policies.

Other Places

Sometimes you end up with a puppy because a dog belonging to your friend or neighbor unexpectedly has a litter, or you find a litter abandoned on the street. While you may be providing such puppies with a better life, they also have a lot of unknowns. You might not know much about the puppy's breed history, exact age, or temperament. Most of the time, you're acquiring the puppy without any formal contract or paperwork, so you have no protection if something goes wrong with the puppy's health or the puppy isn't a good fit for your family. Having a health exam done by a veterinarian is the most important first step before bringing your puppy home.

Chapter Two: Choosing a Blue Lacy

Checking the Health Status

While a puppy's health status can never be guaranteed, you can look for signs that your prospective puppy is in good health while you're visiting them in a familiar environment before adopting. Do they move normally, or do they stumble and not use all four paws properly? Are they engaging with the other puppies and you, or are they lying quietly by themselves? The puppy should have a good appetite and normal energy levels without signs of lethargy, no discharge or redness in the eyes or nose, and clean ears that are free of wax or debris. Check the puppy's coat to ensure it's free of dirt and detritus, with no obvious odor. Ask if the puppy has been experiencing any coughing, sneezing, vomiting, or diarrhea.

If you do select a puppy who shows signs of potential health problems, make sure you're prepared for the financial responsibility that will accompany them. Have your puppy checked by a vet right away, ideally before you even bring them home, in case their condition is contagious to you or other animals. For many health issues, early intervention can make the difference between a successful recovery and a lengthy medical battle.

Chapter Three: Owning a Blue Lacy

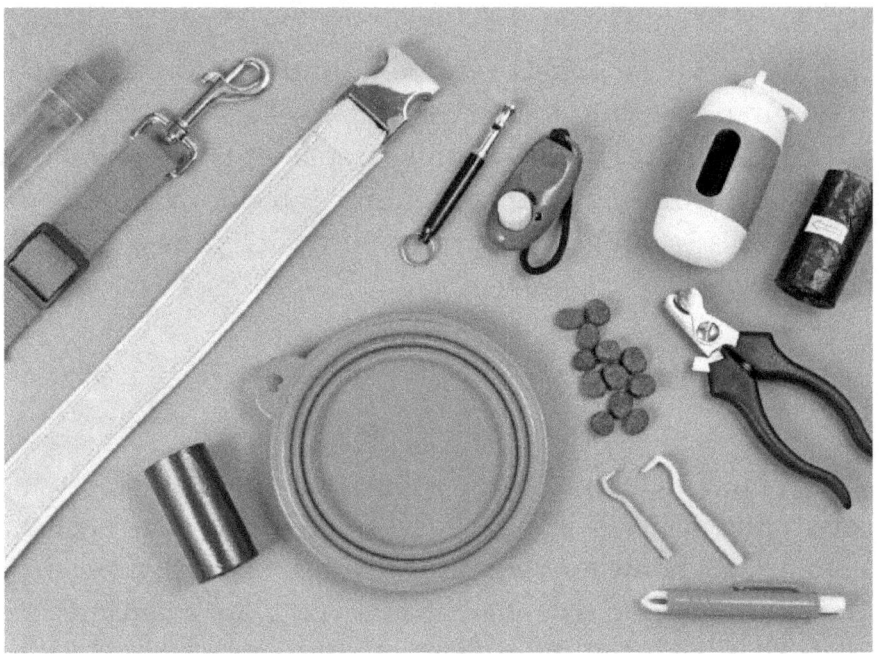

Supplies Needed

Blue Lacy puppies are not cheap, and they require plenty of equipment and tools to ensure that you've got everything that you will need. Now, some things are a matter of personal preference, but you must also be mindful of other times that are required. For example, you need to know what kind of food you are going to feed your pup and how much they need. Of course, these rules are constantly changing as your pup grows. You will need to be prepared prior to get your puppy and bringing him or her home, and for that reason, this chapter will prepare you with a list of everything

Chapter Three: Owning a Blue Lacy

that you will need to have on hand to ensure that your pup has everything necessary.

We will be going over five distinct categories: Dietary, grooming, cleaning, training, and miscellaneous categories. When you make sure that you've got all of the supplies that your pup will need, you are setting yourself up for success. You are also setting your puppy up for success as well.

Living Supplies

First, let's go over your Blue Lacy pup's living environment. This is necessary so that you can create a comfortable home for your pup as well as space that he or she can call their own. For this section, you want to ensure that your pup has everything they will need to be comfortable. Before you start purchasing here, there are a few considerations to keep in mind. Are you planning on crate training? If so, then the crate will be the pup's primary living space. Are you planning on setting your pup up with a section of the home, or a room where they are able to explore? You'll probably want some pens to set that up. Consider the following supplies to ensure that your pup has the best space possible for them.

- **Crate:** If you're crate training, you will need one of these. Keep in mind that to be effective, a crate must be restricted in size. Most people use crates

Chapter Three: Owning a Blue Lacy

in hopes of preventing accidents, but to do that, the crate must be sufficiently small enough to prevent the pup from going in his or her space. A general rule of thumb is that the crate must be tall enough for the pup to stand up comfortably. It must be long enough that the pup can stand straight without touching either end. It must be wide enough for the pup to make a complete turn. Of course, this means that your crate will be quite small for a puppy. Thankfully, many manufacturers, well aware of how rapidly pups can grow and will make crates that are adjustable. This way, you can buy the adult-sized crate and then use dividers to keep it to the proper size, adjusting as necessary as your puppy grows. This is a perfect option if you have a large breed dog, which will change far quicker than a smaller breed.

- **Bedding:** Though this is a bit of a sore subject with very young puppies, bedding provides your pup with somewhere comfy to snuggle up for the night. Your pup may not technically need this, but it is a nice touch. Keep in mind that young puppies may choose to chew on their bed, and you may want to stick to old towels for bedding those first few nights to see how he does with that before placing the bed within the crate.

- **Baby gates:** Depending upon the layout of your home, baby gates are the perfect way to keep your puppy locked up in just certain areas. With baby gates, you will be able to restrict your puppy's space to just the areas that you have prepared and

Chapter Three: Owning a Blue Lacy

puppy-proofed so that you can be certain that your puppy isn't able to access areas that are off-limits.

- **A puppy playpen:** Child-sized playpens often aren't enough for larger breed puppies, especially as they continue to grow. When that happens, you are better off looking to use a puppy pen. These can be significantly taller and are typically made out of steel to prevent your pup from being able to chew through them. They work like portable fences that you can put up just about anywhere to keep your pup where they belong so that you can be certain that they will not get hurt.

Dietary Supplies

Your Blue Lacy pup needs a way to eat and drink, and that's something that is going to be essential in your supplies as well. You must provide your pup with access to fresh food several times per day. Additionally, water should be available most of the time as well, though at first during the earlier months, you can cut down on the overnight potty breaks by taking away the water bowl an hour or two before bed. This is the perfect way to help yourself ensure that your pup won't be waking you up all night long to pee and won't be having accidents. Now, let's go over the checklist of dietary supplies that you will need.

- **Food and water bowls:** Your pup should have two bowls—one for food and one for water. Ideally,

Chapter Three: Owning a Blue Lacy

they would be non-tip, unless you enjoy dealing with the constant mess when your puppy learns that they can flip the bowl over. These bowls should provide your pup with enough food for the serving size they need at that point in time. Check the weight charts for feeding directions for the puppy's food of choice and then make sure that your food bowl can accommodate at least that.

- **Food:** Your pup will need to be transitioned to whatever brand that you would like him to eat. This means that at first, you will need to get the food that the breeder was using so that you can slowly make the transition by taking the time to create ratios of the new food. For example, you would start with a 1:4 ratio of new food to old food, mixed well, for every feeding. This gives your pup time to adjust to the new food without any tummy upset that you might be likely to encounter otherwise.

- **Vitamins:** It's always a good idea to provide your pup with some delicious vitamins that you can use to ensure that he or she gets everything that they need. This can be done the most effectively by ensuring that you understand the breed and what they need. Does your pup have a double coat? You might want to consider some salmon oil to help it come in nice and evenly. Do you have a dog that's

Chapter Three: Owning a Blue Lacy

a bit older? It could be time to introduce some glucosamine treats to help their joints.

- **Chewing treats:** Of course, you should always have treats on hand as well. Puppies can be quite destructive if left to their own devices, and because of that, it is a good idea to have some treat options that can keep them busy. One such example is bully sticks. These treats can be used to keep your pup busy for hours as he gnashes away at the stick, leaving you more capable of focusing on other things as well. Of course, if you are feeding your pup this kind of treat, it is a good idea to supervise him the whole time.

- **Teeth cleaning treats:** Though this could technically fall under grooming, we will touch upon teeth cleaning treats here. Not all dogs are willing to let you brush their teeth. You should absolutely try and do so regularly, but if you have a stubborn dog, another way that you can ensure that his or her teeth are maintained well is to provide them with teeth cleaning treats. These will typically cause your pup's teeth to sink into the treat, cleaning them as they chew them up.

Cleaning Supplies

Chapter Three: Owning a Blue Lacy

Your Blue Lacy pup will inevitably make messes, and there will be very little that you can do about it. Puppies rarely are perfectly potty trained when you get them, especially if you bought from a breeder, and you got your pup around the 8-week mark. At this age, they're still learning about their world and how to navigate it. They are also on the young end to be able to fully control their bladders. As a result, you run into plenty of accidents. This is another reason that you should keep your pup contained at first—it means that there is less space for messes to occur. Now, some pups and breeds are more fastidious than others, but you can expect accidents in some way or another. For that reason, you should consider keeping the following on hand:

- **Enzyme spray:** You will want to make sure that any accidents are immediately treated with an enzyme spray. This is necessary to ensure that the scent is completely destroyed. When pups are learning to potty train, they tend to sniff about to find the place where they are allowed to go. They use the scent of previous messes for cueing them to go, so if they pee on your favorite rug and you never properly treat it, you run the risk that your rug will now be the designated potty spot no matter how often you try to get them to stop.

- **Vacuum and carpet cleaner:** If you have carpet, it's time for you to start vacuuming regularly. Not only will this stop your pup from finding little bits and pieces all over the floor, but you will also be

Chapter Three: Owning a Blue Lacy

able to do a deeper clean if your pup has an accident. A carpet cleaner makes sure that you can get deep into the carpet to keep it clean, also aiding in deodorizing the carpet.

- **Puppy pads:** You may want to consider covering the ground where you keep your puppy with puppy pads. This will make cleanup a breeze because you won't have to worry so much about what to do. The carpet will be protected, and all you will have to do is pick up the soiled pads and replace them.

Grooming Supplies

Many dogs will require some degree of grooming. Some may need more than others—for example, if you have a long-haired dog, you will probably need to brush their hair out daily, much as you would do for yourself. If you have a shorter haired dog, you might just need a small comb or brush to knock out some of the loose furs. Let's go over the most basic grooming supplies that you will need

- **Puppy shampoo and conditioner:** Make sure that any shampoo and conditioner that you choose to use is approved for puppies. This is so that you do not irritate their sensitive fur or eyes as you wash them.

Chapter Three: Owning a Blue Lacy

- **Deshedding brush:** This will be dependent upon the breed that you have chosen, so do your research and choose accordingly.

- **Grooming wipes:** Most dogs are not supposed to be bathed regularly, and some even keep themselves mostly clean on their own without your intervention being needed at all. With those dogs, sometimes, all you need is a quick grooming wipe or two to wipe up any dirt or muck that is dirtying your pup so that you don't have to drop them in the entire bath.

- **Nail clippers:** You need to keep your pup's nails trimmed, especially if you live somewhere that they are not going to be walking on cement regularly. Cement will help to keep the nails ground down so that you don't really have to worry about the length of them. They will naturally shorten over time. However, if you don't live in the city or you don't intend to walk in the city, you may need to clip your pup's nails.

- **Nail grinder:** After you've clipped those nails, next comes grinding them down so that you've got a nice, rounded finish without jagged edges. Some

Chapter Three: Owning a Blue Lacy

people prefer a manual file, but you can't go wrong with a puppy-specific Dremel that will keep your pup's nails in tip-top condition. Just make sure that the Dremel that you choose to use has a guard on it so that you don't accidentally grind away too much of the nail or hurt your pup's paws.

- **Toothbrush and toothpaste:** Yes, you should be brushing your pup's teeth regularly, and the best way to do this is to get him or her used to it from an early age. If they dislike the entire toothbrush, you can make use of a fingertip toothbrush, which you then rub along your pup's teeth.

Training Supplies

Training supplies are also a must-have when it comes to your Blue Lacy pup. Most of the time, people use treats along with a clicker to ensure that the pups get the message. Let's take a look at what you will want to have on hand for training:

- **Treats:** Offering your pup treats is the perfect way to bribe them into obeying you when you try to get them to do something. This is how you teach them. You teach them with the treat itself, carefully using it to guide the motion that you want, and then you reinforce that motion and command with a treat.

Chapter Three: Owning a Blue Lacy

Over time, the pup will pick up, and you will be able to train with less and less treat reinforcement. If you don't want to use special treats, you can often just offer bits of your pup's food as the treat instead.

- **Treat pouch:** Your pup, early on, is going to need to be with you at just about any time, and you want to reinforce them any time they do something right. For this reason, you should keep a pouch that you can clip to your belt or pocket. Or, you could even just keep a pocketful of treats at all times as well if you would prefer. The choice is yours.

- **Clicker:** If you choose to clicker train, you will want to invest in one of these, which you will keep everywhere. However, you can just as easily train your pup with a verbal command as you can with a clicker.

Miscellaneous Supplies

Now, it's time to go over everything that your pup could possibly need that has to yet been covered. There are plenty of tools and supplies that you will need beyond what has already been listed that don't quite fall into any of the above categories. These are tools that still matter, however, and you will want to keep them on hand.

Chapter Three: Owning a Blue Lacy

- **Collar and leash:** At the bare minimum, your puppy will need a collar that you can clip a name tag and rabies verification to. You will also need a leash to walk your dog.

- **Harness:** Some people swear by a harness to help them to control their dog. This works because when you put your pup in a harness, if they pull, they are putting pressure against their chest instead of their neck. This prevents them from painful choking, which could teach them that they should always avoid leashes instead of being happy to walk on them.

- **Chew toys:** Your pup will chew. A lot. Make sure that you always redirect to toys that are allowed to be chewed on so that you can prevent him from feeling like he can chew on just anything that he finds. By constantly redirecting to his chew toys, he will learn.

- **No-chew spray:** Some people swear by this. They spritz the things that their puppy has been chewing on with a no-chew spray, and as a result, they find that they are much more likely to stop chewing on things that they shouldn't be.

Chapter Three: Owning a Blue Lacy

- **Toys to stimulate the mind:** Make sure that your pup has plenty of toys. Remember that a tired dog is a happy dog, and because of that, you want to make sure that your pup is always running and playing to prevent him or her from being too destructive.

Puppy-proofing Your Home

The first step that must happen before your Blue Lacy pup comes home is to ensure that your home is puppy-proof. Just as you would baby-proof if you were welcoming a baby home, you must ensure that you prepare. However, Blue Lacy puppies are completely mobile as soon as you bring them home. They are more than capable of walking, scratching, and chewing through just about anything that you leave within their reach, which means that you must prepare before the puppy comes home. Now, let's look at several simple steps to puppy-proofing.

Step 1: Hide the trash

Your trash needs to be well out of reach for your pup. While not all puppies will decide that the trash can is the perfect play area, there can be all sorts of smells that are enticing to your new pup that convince him or her to start fishing inside of it. Because they are likely to be attracted to the garbage in some way, shape, or form, you must make sure

Chapter Three: Owning a Blue Lacy

that the garbage can is protected. Block it beyond a baby gate, for example, so your puppy can't get to it. You could also get one that has a top that your puppy won't be able to knock loose.

Step 2: Cover and contain cords

Puppies often are given toys to play with and chew on at are long, thin, and somewhat rope-like. Think of how may chewy ropes that you may have on hand right now—a lot of people love them to play with their puppy. They create a great playing opportunity for your pup. Unfortunately, they may also quickly think that anything that is long, thin, and flexible becomes a great source of entertainment, leading to your pup going straight for any wires that they may happen to stumble upon as they go about their day. However, these are dangerous. Not only could they shock themselves, you have to worry about them swallowing the bits that they chew up too, which is also dangerous in their own way. Give your pup something that is chewing-friendly instead so they can learn to associate new toys with being approved upon to chew.

Step 3: put bags and purses away

A lot of the time, we forget about our bags, purses, and other things that we use to carry our stuff around. However, diaper bags, purses, and the like, usually contain a treasure trove of dangerous items that could potentially harm your

Chapter Three: Owning a Blue Lacy

pup. Items that might seem harmless, like chewing gum, for example, actually contain Xylitol, which is highly toxic for dogs. Additionally, any medication that you may have in your purse is designed for ratios that are effective for people, not animals, and that means that your meds could be highly dangerous for a tiny puppy. The best way to avoid these problems is to just keep all bags and purses out of your pup's reach.

Step 4: Be mindful of houseplants

Did you know that there are several houseplants that are actually toxic to puppies? These plants can cause you several problems if your pup manages to reach them, and therefore, if you plan on bringing home a puppy, you must make sure that you have the right kinds of plants around. The most dangerous plants that you can have around your pup include:

- Sago palms
- Castor bean
- American yew
- American crocus

If you have these plants at home, make sure that they are well out of reach from your pup. If you don't have these plants, plan to keep it that way for the benefit of your pup.

Chapter Three: Owning a Blue Lacy

Step 5: Set some space aside that's his or hers

Just as every other member of your family needs somewhere to retreat to as necessary, your pup needs somewhere that they can go to protect themselves and relax. This is sort of like giving them their own room—you set them somewhere that they can be safe and happy, and as a result, they know when they want to be left alone, they can retreat there as well. The most common method of doing so is with a crate. There are pros and cons to create training, and we will be going over those shortly.

Step 6: Lock up the poisons

Just as you should do to protect your inquisitive toddlers from exploring in that cabinet under the sink to see what's inside, you must also lock up your poisons from your dog as well. You don't want your pup to chew up some poisons, which may be tasty to entice mice or rats to consume them to kill them. You must make sure that these are all out of reach, even if that is attained simply by setting up so that there is a childproof lock covering up the door to the cabinet where you store everything.

Step 7: Limit movements

Chapter Three: Owning a Blue Lacy

Your puppy will want to explore your home, but until he or she knows your rules and what to expect, you want to limit just how much space your pup has to do so. You want to ensure that you've restricted your pup to just one room, or even half of a room, at first before slowly expanding upon his or her world as you get to better know their limits and what you can expect from them. You can do this by making sure that doors stay closed or by installing baby gates and pens to block him or her from those rooms that they shouldn't be in.

Step 8: Limit heights

Your pup's bones are still quite fragile, and because of this, you want to make sure that they aren't in positions where they can easily jump and get hurt. Even leaping off of the couch to the ground could be too much, depending upon the breed and the size. You want to try to keep your pup at ground level as much as possible for this reason—you want them to avoid jumping as much as possible while their joints are still developing to be certain that your puppy isn't going to accidentally hurt themselves.

Step 9: Be mindful of batteries

A lot of people forget about battery-operated toys. Whether you have a battery-operated toy for your pup or you have children who tend to forget about where they put the remote, you want to be mindful. Nothing would stop a puppy from chewing up that remote into little pieces, with the battery included on the menu. However, batteries are full of battery acid, and that's no good for your pets. Find a good place for your remote, and keep it there. Additionally, make sure that there are no batteries that your pup can easily reach so that you can be certain your puppy isn't going to end up making themselves sick.

Dealing with Separation Anxiety

When a Blue Lacy dog is separated from its first family and taken to a new home, they may howl and whine. Even once settled in they sometimes continue to do so when left alone.

This is completely normal and happens as a result of their instinctive fear that they are being abandoned by their pack. By howling and whining they are effectively sounding the alarm so that someone will come to the rescue.

Now, no matter how heart wrenching this is, coming to the rescue is exactly what you should not make a habit of doing.

The first course of action here is to get your dog accustomed to being left alone. Even when you are home it is good practice to spend some time apart so that when you do leave the house they don't become stressed or scared.

Chapter Three: Owning a Blue Lacy

Here's a step-by-step drill to deal with separation anxiety:

1. Start by settling your dog down in his or her own area, bed or crate.
2. Offer a small treat before departing for a short while. If he or she cries out do not be tempted to rush back and offer reassurance as this will train them to believe they can get your attention by howling or whining.
3. Wait until they quiet down and then go back to offer a reward for this good behavior. If your dog continues to cry out then sternly tell them 'no!' and wait until they have stopped to interact with them again.
4. Gradually increase the time you leave them alone until they are comfortable with it.

If a dog howls or whines incessantly when left alone then they probably aren't comfortable in their surroundings yet, so spend a bit of extra time getting them accustomed to it by socializing with them there throughout the day. Be sure to offer plenty of praise and affection as well as the odd treat while doing so.

Tip: Place a puzzle toy with a treat stuffed inside into your dog's confinement area. This will teach them to associate this place with fun and food while also distracting them from the fact that you may have left them alone.

Please note that if your dog howls or whines for prolonged periods or at strange times despite regular training then it may not be due to separation anxiety. In these cases, it is always best to seek advice from a veterinarian to ensure there is no underlying issue.

Chapter Three: Owning a Blue Lacy

Chapter Four: Nutrition for Blue Lacy

Nutrition is important for your growing Blue Lacy puppy, and the mass of dog food options on the market can be overwhelming. This chapter will cover the basics of what your Blue Lacy puppy needs to grow healthy and strong while also helping you choose feeding options that fit your lifestyle.

What to Feed Your Puppy

There are a few different ways to approach feeding your puppy, and each has its advantages and disadvantages. This section will guide you through your decision-

Chapter Four: Nutrition for Blue Lacy

making process, helping you choose the best option for your puppy and you. It's important to select a pet food based on your puppy's age and phase of growth, keeping any medical concerns in mind. Consult with your veterinarian about your food selection to ensure it meets your puppy's needs.

Dry Kibble

Kibble is the most common choice for feeding Blue Lacy puppies and adult dogs. It's low-cost, has a long shelf life, and doesn't require any special storage. It also has the added benefit of massaging your puppy's gums and teeth to a degree, which can contribute to improved oral health. There is a large variety of options available on the market, but not all are equally appropriate for your Blue Lacy puppy.

When choosing a kibble brand, check first for an AAFCO certification label on the bag. This indicates that the product has undergone testing and feeding trials by the Association of American Feed Control Officials and has been deemed balanced and appropriate for use.

Next, consider the ingredient list on the back of the bag. Dogs, unlike cats, are not strict carnivores. Plant-based ingredients like grains, fruits, and vegetables are not just dietary fillers; they contain important vitamins, minerals, and fiber that contribute to your puppy's overall health and development. That said, a protein should be one of the first three ingredients listed.

Chapter Four: Nutrition for Blue Lacy

You'll also want to research the manufacturer and company to ensure you're buying a reputable brand with good quality-control measures. Veterinary-exclusive brands, such as Medi-Cal, Hill's, or Science Diet, are among my top brand recommendations for their rigorous research, feeding trials, and quality-control practices, but there are plenty of other great options out there.

Wet Food

Wet, or canned, food often has the same ingredients as kibble but in different ratios. For example, wet food is of course much higher in water than kibble. Canned food is packaged in durable containers and generally has a long shelf life, but once it's opened, it must be refrigerated and fed to your puppy within a few days or it'll go bad. Wet food is often more palatable to dogs, so it may be a better choice for a picky eater. However, it's also more expensive than kibble. If you're looking to both save money and add flavor, try mixing a few tablespoons of a yummy wet food in with your dog's kibble at each meal instead of feeding them wet food alone.

Raw Food

Although it may be an option to look into when your dog is older, raw diets are not recommended for puppies. It's very important for them to get enough calcium and phosphorus as they grow, and if the raw diet is not appropriately balanced, it can result in bone deformities and growth issues.

There are also some major health risks to consider. There's no guarantee that these products are free of dangerous pathogens, such as Salmonella or E. coli, which can cause vomiting, diarrhea, fevers, and occasionally death for dogs. If you or your kids accidentally ingest bacteria like these when preparing and feeding raw meals, when your puppy licks you, or even when scooping your puppy's poop, you could suffer the same consequences.

Special Diets

Some puppies and dogs have special needs when it comes to what they can and cannot eat. For example, if your puppy has frequent indigestion, your vet might prescribe a gastrointestinal (GI) diet, which is designed to be bland and easily digestible but still nutritionally balanced. (Make sure to buy a puppy formula to continue supporting development.)

Your puppy might also need a special diet if they're allergic to certain foods, like chicken, beef, dairy, or eggs. (Grains and other plant-based foods are less common allergens.) If your dog has itchy or infected skin, ear infections, or gastrointestinal distress, they might have allergies—or they might have parasites or another illness, so

Chapter Four: Nutrition for Blue Lacy

be sure to visit your vet. It's difficult to test animals for allergies reliably. The most common technique is a dietary elimination trial in which you feed your dog only foods that do not contain the suspected allergen for eight weeks and monitor the results. For example, if you completely remove beef from your dog's diet and notice that their skin gets less red and itchy, your dog may have a sensitivity to beef proteins, and you should only feed them food without beef or beef products (including beef-flavored treats and medications). A vet can help you keep your dog comfortable during a food trial by treating any underlying infections and making sure you aren't inadvertently feeding them the wrong foods. Note that trials can be difficult if you have kids at home, as they may be prone to dropping food on the ground or feeding the dog without your knowledge.

Water

Drinking enough water is just as important for dogs as it is for humans, so your puppy needs access to fresh, clean water daily. Puppies generally require one ounce of water per pound of body weight each day, but that can vary depending on how hot it is outside and how much the dog has exercised. Keep a dish of water in an easily accessible area of your home, ideally one where your puppy spends a lot of time. Rinse the bowl and replace the water daily to keep it free of gross buildup and dirt, and wash it with soap and water at least once a week.

Chapter Four: Nutrition for Blue Lacy

If you're worried that your puppy may be dehydrated, speak to your veterinarian. Signs of dehydration include dry or tacky gums, sunken or dry eyes, or a persistent "skin tent" (when you pull up the puppy's scruff and it takes several seconds to return to normal). There are some ways you can encourage your puppy to drink more water, such as feeding them wet food or adding a small amount of low-sodium chicken or beef broth to their water.

Supplements

There are many nutritional supplements on the market for dogs, and it can be confusing to know what exactly your dog needs. Common supplements that address specific medical conditions include joint supplements such as glucosamine for adult or senior dogs and fish oils or omega-3 fatty acids to support dry, dull, or itchy skin.

If you're feeding your puppy an appropriate and nutritionally balanced diet, there is usually no need for supplements. Consult with your vet before adding one to your puppy's diet to be certain it's safe and effective. You might need pharmaceuticals to properly address a medical concern, but supplements can often support the treatment or help prevent the problem from reoccurring. And make sure you follow your vet's or the product's guidelines and use the right dose for your puppy's age and weight.

Human Food

Chapter Four: Nutrition for Blue Lacy

It may be tempting to offer your puppy human food, but there are some things to consider first. Remember, if you're feeding your puppy a nutritionally balanced dog food, human food is not needed to support their nutritional health—it probably just adds calories and fats to their daily intake. Many human foods are too rich for puppies, which can result in an upset stomach, vomiting, or diarrhea. And some human foods are unsafe or even toxic for dogs. Avoid foods with sauces or spices, since it can be difficult to know exactly what the ingredients are.

List of Approved Foods and their Nutrients

Foods Approved for Dogs	Nutrients
Cantaloupe	B6, Vitamin C, niacin, folate, fiber, and potassium
Green Beans	Calcium, fiber, copper, folic acid, potassium, thiamin, riboflavin, iron, manganese, and niacin

Chapter Four: Nutrition for Blue Lacy

Spinach	Iron, Vitamin A, Vitamin C, and potassium
Apples	Vitamin C and antioxidants
Pumpkin	Vitamin A, fiber, and antioxidants
Sweet Potatoes	Vitamins C, A, B6 and E, folate, iron, calcium, iron, potassium, thiamine, and copper
Blueberries	Resveratrol, thiamine, potassium and Vitamin C
Watermelon	Lycopene, Vitamins B6, A and C and thiamin
Asparagus	Vitamins C, E, B1, B2, A, K, fiber, copper, folate, iron, potassium, and manganese

Chapter Four: Nutrition for Blue Lacy

Brussels Sprouts	Vitamins B1, B6, K and A, fiber, potassium, folate manganese and riboflavin
Lettuce	Vitamin A
Cucumber	Potassium, Vitamin A, C, K and phosphorus
Celery	Potassium, Calcium, Magnesium, Selenium, Phosphorus, Vitamin A and K and thiamin
Cauliflower	Potassium, Sodium, Vitamin C, and folate
Cabbage	Vitamin C and K and folate, Potassium, calcium, and Magnesium
Bell Pepper	Vitamin C and A and potassium
Broccoli	Vitamin C, A and K, riboflavin, potassium, magnesium, and sodium

Chapter Four: Nutrition for Blue Lacy

Banana	Vitamin A, thiamine, riboflavin and potassium
Strawberries	Vitamin A, C, niacin, potassium, phosphorus, and calcium
Pear	Folate, Pantothenic Acid, Magnesium, and potassium -
Orange	Vitamin C, A, folate and calcium and potassium
Peanut Butter (unsalted and no xylitol)	Protein, Vitamins E, B, niacin and healthy fat
Chicken (cooked)	Protein
Baby Carrots	Fiber and Vitamin A

Chapter Four: Nutrition for Blue Lacy

Eggs	Protein, selenium, and riboflavin
Oatmeal (cooked)	Fiber
Pork, Beef, and Lamb (cooked)	Zinc, selenium, potassium, iron, magnesium, folic acid chromium, copper, Vitamins K, D, B and A and protein
Fish	Vitamin B6, B12, and C, Omega-3, phosphorus and protein

List of Toxic Foods for Blue Lacy

Raisins
Grapes
Onion
Garlic
Cherries

Chapter Four: Nutrition for Blue Lacy

Mushrooms
Currants
Green and Raw Potatoes
Raw Meat
Raw Eggs
Candy
Tea
Avocado
Alcohol Beverages
Sugary Foods
Peanut Butter (Xylitol)
Yeast Dough
Raw Fish
Apricot
Rhubarb
Apple Seeds
Tomato Plants
Chocolate
Fatty Meat and Bacon

Chapter Four: Nutrition for Blue Lacy

Salty Food
Dairy Products (except yogurt)
Moldy Foods
Coffee

Chapter Four: Nutrition for Blue Lacy

Chapter Five: Raising and Training a Blue Lacy

The Top Commands to Teach Your Blue Lacy Puppy

This chapter is where we get to some of the fun stuff about training! We are going to look at some of the steps that you can take in order to teach your puppy some basic commands. There are a lot of different commands that you are able to teach your puppy, but we are going to focus on some of the basic ones that will make your life with your puppy a little bit easier. Some of the basic commands that we need to take a look at include:

Chapter Five: Raising and Training a Blue Lacy

Sit

Teaching your Blue Lacy puppy how to sit can be a stepping stone to making sure that the puppy is a well-trained dog. When the puppy can sit on command, it helps them to learn some self-control. This method of teaching your puppy to sit is going to teach them how to sit down physically but can be a good way for the puppy to learn how to calm down mentally and engage their focus on you. Before you try moving on to any other trick or command, make sure that your puppy has mastered sitting. Some steps that you can use to help with the teaching of the sit command includes:

1. Have the puppy face you. Tell the puppy to "sit" while you hold out a treat in the hand position of your choice.
2. After saying sit once, you are not going to repeat the word again.
3. Put the treat to the nose of your puppy.
4. Move the hand so that it goes slowly forward, from the direction you are in, towards the dog as if you are going to move the treat over the head of the puppy.
    a. The reason that we do this is that it is an automatic way to get the puppy to lower their butt as they try to get to the treat.
5. Once the puppy has their butt on the floor, you can reward them using the treat and the clicker word.
6. During this process, it is important for you to go at the pace of your puppy, and you need to keep the treat on their nose. Also, never force the puppy to

Chapter Five: Raising and Training a Blue Lacy

sit down by pushing their butt onto the floor. This isn't going to teach the puppy anything since you are forcing it, and it can cause some harm to the hips of the puppy if you are too forceful.
7. In the next fifteen to twenty minutes, repeat this exercise as many times as the puppy will do it to help reinforce the command.

As you go through this process, do not start to feel discouraged if the puppy is not sitting down the first time you do it. Some puppies don't realize what is going on and that they need to lower their butt to get the treat. But patience and persistence is the best way for you to get them to start listening to you. If the puppy starts to give up on the treat and doesn't seem like they are focused any longer, saying their name or using a kissy noise can be a good way to get their attention back on you.

Lay Down

After you and your Blue Lacy have worked on the sit command for a bit, and the puppy has got this part mastered, it is time to move on to the second command of lay down. You must make sure that the puppy knows how to sit before you start working with the lay down command because if you start teaching them too many commands at once, then you are just going to add confusion to the mix.

Chapter Five: Raising and Training a Blue Lacy

When the Blue Lacy puppy is ready to learn how to lay down, get them to sit in front of you. Next, hold the treat in one hand, and then using the other hand, signal the puppy to lay down by using a hand gesture that had your pointer finger pointing down to the ground in front of the puppy's face. Some of the other steps that you need to use to work on the laying down command include:

1. Put the treat that you are using up to the nose of the puppy and then start to slowly lure the puppy down. You can do this by moving the hand down to the floor, somewhere between their paws. Go at the pace for your dog.
2. Once your hand with the treat hits the floor, slowly move it towards you and away from him along the floor. This motion should be enough to get the dog to lower themselves into a laying position.
3. Once you are able to get the puppy to lay down all of the way, make sure to say the clicker word and give them a treat.
4. Repeat this exercise as many times as you can in the next 15 minutes to help the puppy get the idea down.

Keep in mind with this one that the laying down command is going to force your puppy to focus a bit longer before they are able to get the treat that they want. There are going to be times when the puppy wants to give up before you are able to finish with the final position. Don't get frustrated with this; just

Chapter Five: Raising and Training a Blue Lacy

keep trying, and your puppy will start to catch on to what you want them to do.

Stay

Teaching your puppy how to stay where you want, even when they want to run off and do something else, is a great training tool that you should work on once the puppy learns how to sit and lay down. It is also a command that can take some time to learn, so bring on the patience. Think of how much self-control you have to teach to a small puppy and how long they need to maintain their attention span in order to actually stay put when you want them to.

There are different methods that you can use for this one, but sometimes it is easiest to get the puppy to stay when you have them in the lay down position. This means that they are going to be less likely to want to move when they can lay all the way down rather than sitting, but you definitely can teach this command in either position.

The hand position that we need to work with for the stay command is to put your hand up, palm facing the puppy, and fingers together. Think of the hand position that you would use when trying to stop someone from coming towards you. Once you have the hand position and have used the command "stay" to the puppy, the other steps to this process that you need to follow includes:

Chapter Five: Raising and Training a Blue Lacy

1. With your hand out, take a step back using both feet.
2. After the two steps back, return back to the position you were at to start.
3. If your puppy was good and stayed seated that entire time, reward them with a treat and with the clicker word.
    a. Keep in mind that this is a puppy, and they probably will not want to stay still. If your puppy does get up before you can return to them, tell them "uh-uh" and get them to go back into the seated position.
    b. For the first few sessions, this may be as far as you are able to get. And that is just fine. The puppy naturally wants to follow you. Just work with them until you can get them to stay seated the whole time.
4. Once the puppy stays seated, try taking two steps back and then returning before the reward and the clicker word.
5. Keep increasing the distance that you decide to walk away from the pup, seeing how long you can go away before they start getting up again. Do this until the puppy starts to understand the command that you are giving them.
6. Repeat this exercise many times until the puppy learns how to stay put.

Wait

Chapter Five: Raising and Training a Blue Lacy

After you are done teaching your puppy how to stay, it is time to teach them how to wait. This is a very useful command that you can work with, but often it is underused. It can be applied to teaching your puppy to wait for their food, wait to get their leash off, wait to get out of the crate, and more. It is a great way to teach your puppy a bit of self-control and patience, which is something that all dog owners need at some point or another.

Teaching self-control to the puppy is going to be the key to having a dog that is well trained and can do a great job with all the areas of obedience. Definitely take some time to teach your puppy how to listen to this command. When you are ready to start with, it put the puppy in the position that you would like them to wait in. You may find that sitting or lying down is going to work for this. The best hand signals to use here is to have your pointer finger going up. The steps that you can use to make this happen includes:

1. Tell your puppy to wait and then use the wait hand signal.
2. While the puppy is in the seated position, preferably in the crate where feedings are supposed to happen, slowly lower the food bowl down to where they can eat.
3. If the puppy sees the bowl of food and starts to jump up or get at the food in other ways, you raise the bowl back up while saying "uh-uh."
4. Get the puppy back into the seated position and then start again. If the puppy is younger or has a

Chapter Five: Raising and Training a Blue Lacy

lot of energy, you may have to repeat these steps a few times in order to get them to listen to you.
   a. Do not set the bowl of food all the way down until the puppy has actually patiently waited for you to lower it without them getting away from the seated position. Be aware that this can take a bit of time.
5. After you have been able to set the food bowl down, see if you are able to get the puppy to wait for another second, and then say, "OK."
   a. If you see that the puppy starts to go for the food before you say the word "OK," you can tell them "uh-uh" and pick up the bowl before trying again.
   b. "OK" is going to be the release word for your puppy, and it will tell them that it is now fine to stop waiting, and they can eat the food that is in front of them.
   c. As you go through this process, you will want to lengthen the amount of time that the puppy is going to wait between setting the bowl down and saying OK. This takes a bit longer but will get the puppy used to waiting until you give the orders to do something.

Come

The next command that we are going to look at is the one to come. When you do this one, you are going to teach your puppy how to come when you call them. This is also one that a lot of pet owners are going to forget to teach, and it can

Chapter Five: Raising and Training a Blue Lacy

lead to some issues with the puppy not listening to you. This is a foundational command that you should work with your puppy on for years to come. You may use it to keep the puppy near you, when there is danger, and more.

Be prepared for this one to take a bit longer than some of the other ones. The puppy has to let you move away from them and then has to move to meet you. There are a number of steps that this will entail working with, but this is a great one to focus your attention on and make sure that you can get them to really listen to you. When you are ready to teach your puppy this command, you can follow these steps:

1. When you are working with this command, make sure that you start out in an enclosed area. This makes it easier in case your puppy decides not to listen because they are limited in the space they have to run away.
2. Take your puppy off the leash and allow them to have some time to just explore and roam around.
3. When you are ready, say the name of the puppy and then use the command "Come" in a positive voice while also holding on to a treat.
    a. Keep in mind that you want to associate this command with positivity.
    b. Your goal is to get the dog to come every time that you call them. For this to happen, the puppy needs to be conditioned to think that something positive is going to happen when they come to you.

Chapter Five: Raising and Training a Blue Lacy

4. If your puppy doesn't end up coming over to you right away, that is fine. You can make some kissy noises or do another thing that will get their attention to make sure that they see the treat that you are offering. Be patient here and work on redirecting the attention of the puppy until he comes to you.
5. When the puppy does come to you, make sure that you reward them with the treat, as well as the clicker word. Do this even if it took a long time for the puppy to make their way over to you. They did listen, even if it took longer than you wanted.
6. Repeat this exercise many times until the puppy starts to come right over to you.

Leave It

The next command that we need to take a look at is "leave it." This can be a beneficial command to train your puppy, considering that they often like to be adventurous and get into everything. When you decide to use this command when the puppy is heading towards something that you don't want them to be in, you are going to see some great results. As the puppy wants to explore and see things, there are many times when this kind of command is going to be a good one to use.

Now, there are going to be a few methods that you are able to use when it comes to the command of "leave it." The

Chapter Five: Raising and Training a Blue Lacy

first method is going to follow the steps below to make things happen.

1. Any time that the puppy starts to go for, or is already into something that you want them to leave alone, firmly tell the puppy, "leave it."
2. Remember to only tell them the command once. You can use their name or another sound to get their attention.
3. If you find that the puppy is not responding to this, put a treat or some other toy on their nose and lure them over to listening to you.
4. Once the puppy does decide to leave the object, tell them "Yes" and use the clicker word of your choice. A reward is a good way to reinforce this idea, as well.
5. Remember that your reward for this one needs to be really motivating. You are trying to get the puppy to leave something alone that they are interested in. If the reward is not good, then they are more likely to ignore you and go after the other thing.

The above method is going to work well for most puppies, and it is definitely one you can work with. But another option that you may want to try working with as well, depending on your puppy and whether or not they respond to the first method, is the second method we will tell you about below:

Chapter Five: Raising and Training a Blue Lacy

1. Have the puppy start this training session by lying down.
2. Put down a treat on the ground, covering it with your hand if necessary.
3. Tell your pup to "leave it."
4. Once the puppy looks at you rather than the treat, tell them "Yes" and reward them with the treat from the other hand.
5. Remember, you need to practice this one a bit. It is going to help the dog realize that if they leave the first thing, they are going to get something better, which makes them respond better to you.

Touch

Touch can be a great command to work with, and it is almost like a trick that you are able to do with your puppy. Touch is going to be a great way to teach your puppy to target something and then touch it with their nose. It is a good way to get the brain of your puppy to move and even to keep their focus when it is needed. Some of the steps that you are going to be able to use in order to teach your puppy how to respond to the touch command will include:

1. Make sure that you sit down with the puppy facing you.
2. Hold a treat or some other reward in your one hand.
3. Command your dog to "Touch" and then hold out the hand that doesn't have the treat, so it is flat in front of the nose of your dog while holding onto the treat in the other hand.

Chapter Five: Raising and Training a Blue Lacy

    a. Once the puppy starts to get the hang of this kind of command, it will no longer be necessary to have the treat in your hand, and you can just put the hand where you would like.
4. In the beginning, you want to put the touching hand six inches or so away from the nose of your dog.
5. As soon as you are able to get the nose of your dog to touch your hand, you can reward him with the treat you have and the clicker word you choose to use.
6. You should never give your dog the treat in the hand that you want them to touch.
7. If you find that the dog is getting the hang of this trick pretty quickly, you can remove the treat and no longer use it at all.
8. As you progress with your puppy, keep moving your touching hand higher above the nose of your dog, adding in a bit of difficulty with it.

Shake

Now we are going to move a bit more into some of the different tricks that you are able to do when you work with your puppy. But the way that you do this is going to be pretty similar to the commands that we were doing before. Think of how much fun it is going to be when you want to get your puppy to shake your hand.

Chapter Five: Raising and Training a Blue Lacy

You will find that most puppies are going to take some time to learn how to do this trick. But if you have already spent some time teaching them some of the other commands, it may be a bit easier. As always, your job is to be patient and persistent with this and work on it each day until your puppy is ready to go with it. Some of the steps that you are able to use in order to teach your puppy how to shake with you include:

1. Make sure that you begin this with the puppy facing you.
2. Use the command "shake" and make the shake hand gesture with your hand out, palm out, and waiting.
3. Place the treat right up to one side of your pup's chest.
    a. This one is going to take a bit of patience and can be harder for the puppy to figure out what exactly you want them to do.
    b. Most pups are going to try to bite at the treat and will take some extra pains in order to get to the treat.
4. As soon as the puppy starts to paw at the treat, or even if they just start to lift the paw, immediately reward them with the treat and the clicker word.

For this kind of exercise, if you find that your pup is standing up and getting out of the seated position that you put them in, this is fine. Once they figure out that they are able to get the reward when they lift up their paw, they will figure out

Chapter Five: Raising and Training a Blue Lacy

that it is easier for them to lift up the paw while they are seated. However, when you first start with this exercise, begin it with the puppy in the seated position before you begin.

Heel

The next command that is on our list is going to be heel. Teaching your puppy how to heel can be one of the most beneficial skills that you can teach them. If you are able to focus on this command with them when they are young, they will know how to behave when you get them older. One big behavioral problem that can happen with a puppy or dog when they get older is that they will pull on the leash while walking. Teaching your puppy how to heel is going to avoid this issue and can make walking a bit easier.

Before we get into some of the steps that we need to take in order to teach your puppy how to heel, we need to look at some tips for loose leash walking. First, remember to work with positive reinforcement. You also want to walk with a leash that is loose and never tighten it because this puts some strain on either end of the leash. You also should consider being as consistent as possible with what side your puppy needs to walk on. Pick a side and keep them there.

With these two things in mind, it is time to see how you can teach your puppy when and how to heel at the right time. The steps to making this happen will include:

Chapter Five: Raising and Training a Blue Lacy

1. Position the leash so it is on your arm or wrist, but make sure that it is still a bit loose.
2. If you have the puppy on the right side, make sure to hold onto the end of the leash with your left hand and grab it with the right hand down by your side. If you are holding onto the puppy on the left side, then you can flip these instructions around.
3. If you find that the puppy will stay near your side the whole time, then the second hand on the leash won't be necessary.
4. Get into a position where your puppy is on the side that you choose, and then get their attention.
5. Your goal with this one, if you can, is to get the puppy to be as calm and focused as possible so that they can pay attention to the command that you use. Have the puppy sit by you and then reward with the treat and the clicker word.
6. Say the name of your puppy, and then ask them to "heel." Keep looking at the puppy as you continue to walk.
7. Any time that the puppy looks up at you, you should say the clicker word. Depending on how often the puppy looks at you, you can provide them with a treat with the clicker word or just on occasion.
    a. The more that you see the puppy look up at you, the less you should reward with a treat so that you can slowly wean off this.
8. When it is time, take one step forward and see if you can get the attention of your puppy. Ideally, they are going to stay next to you and will heel rather than trying to pull forward.

Chapter Five: Raising and Training a Blue Lacy

   a. If you find that the puppy is losing their focus on you at any time, say their name or use the kissy noise, but never repeat the command more than once.
   b. If the puppy keeps the focus on you and the leash is loose, keep on walking. If the puppy tightens the leash and pulls forward, then stop with the walking.
9. Your goal here is to get the puppy to walk back over to you and get the leash loose. If the puppy doesn't do this, say their name and get their attention. If they still don't come back to you, take a step back, and see if the puppy will follow you. Last case scenario that they aren't listening to you, then lure them back with a treat.
10. Once the puppy is back to you again, use the clicker word and offer a treat. Repeat this exercise a bunch of times until the puppy is able to learn how to listen to you and do what you are asking with the heeling.

You want to make sure that with this one that you are picking out a treat that your puppy really likes. Your goal with heel is to teach the puppy how to listen to you and stop moving or pulling on the leash. This means that the reward needs to be greater than whatever else may be catching their attention at the time. Go all out with this one and pick out some of the best treats to get the puppy to listen to you.

Chapter Five: Raising and Training a Blue Lacy

There are some puppies who struggle with heel because they are resistant to working with the leash. If this is your puppy, then you should consider working with a harness when teaching the puppy how to heel, and even when you want to introduce them to leash walking in general. Most puppies and older dogs are going to respond to the harness so much better than using the leash for heeling and for working with the leash for walking in any form.

There are a lot of different commands that you are able to work with when it is time to teach your puppy how to listen to you. Most of these are critical commands that can get the puppy to listen to what you want them to do and to keep them out of harm, though a few of them can be almost like fun tricks that you can do together. Make sure that you take your time and go at the speed that works the best for your puppy. They will learn if you are consistent with the treats and continue doing the rewards and the clicker word each time that they succeed in doing what you would like.

Correcting Behavior Problems

Let's face it, there will be a lot of naughtiness around your house, and that is all normal. Puppies have a lot to learn on their way to becoming adult dogs, and that includes testing your limits and pushing the boundaries to see how far you will actually let them go.

Bad behavior is part of the deal of adopting a puppy. You should be aware that it is in your puppy's nature to show

Chapter Five: Raising and Training a Blue Lacy

over excitement in ways you find unacceptable. Just like it is a natural thing to be stressed. It is your job to pin-point the reason for the bad behavior, eradicate the culprit, and completely redirect your puppy with nothing but love and understanding.

Correcting behavioral problems requires time and patience, but approaching the issue with an exaggerated reaction can set both you and your puppy to a path that is much harder to come back from.

Shushing the Barker

Having a constant barker in your home is no fun. Being robbed from your good night's sleep is nothing but a headache. But before you try to find a way to shush your barking ball of fur, you first need to determine what makes your pooch bark in the first place. Barking is a dog's way of communicating, and it is how they express themselves. See what your pooch is trying to tell you before you take a step further:

Barking for Attention

Your puppy just has to go through a phase of not being able to bear being alone. It is a normal part of their development. If your puppy is a loud barker when you are preparing to leave the house, here are some tips that may help you solve the problem:

Chapter Five: Raising and Training a Blue Lacy

- Do not give them attention. By soothing a protester, you only add fuel to the fire. You will not only make things worse, but you will end up with a spoiled pup.
- Do not leave or enter your house in a grandiose way because they are too exciting for your pup and they're only encouraging the barking even more.
- Grab a hollow bone that is safe for your pup to chew on and fill it with some peanut butter. Offer it to your pup before you leave the house to keep them occupied.

You can also try this:

1. Grab an empty can and put it in your pocket.
2. Get ready to leave the house and stand in the hallway.
3. Chances are that your puppy is already barking their lungs out. Throw the can toward (NOT AT your puppy). The goal here is for them to think that this reaction comes from the environment, not you.
4. When your puppy stops barking, give them attention.
5. Do this for every arrival and departure, until it realizes that stopping means getting attention.

Barking at Everything

If your puppy is a real barker, then chances are, nothing in your home goes unnoticed. But, living with

Chapter Five: Raising and Training a Blue Lacy

everlasting barking can be a real pain. If nothing is wrong with them, and you know that it is just an incessant barker, then know that the reason it is doing that is probably because it wants things to go away. For instance, if it barks at a cat, the cat will most likely go away. But if it starts barking at the postman, it may realize that its "superpowers" aren't as effective. So, it will start barking more and more. And then louder and louder.

If your first thought is to try yelling at them to stop (which is quite understandable given that his barking has become the soundtrack of your life), you will only make things worse. To dogs, yelling is the human way of barking. If you start yelling, they will only think you are barking too, and that will lead to – that's right – more barking.

There are three things you can do to try to solve this issue:

1. Start (or intensify) training. Your pooch most likely thinks it is the leader and gets ego boosts as he is probably thinking that it is his duty to guard the territory. By starting or devoting to a more intense training routine, you will let them know it is actually you who is in charge of the home and that there are some rules to be followed.

2. Block off lookout posts. If your pup spends a lot of time in front of the window, guarding and keeping eye on things, make sure to block his access. If necessary, crate them more or secure them with a lead long enough for them just to lie down comfortably. Increase freedom gradually as your pooch becomes less interested in barking.

Chapter Five: Raising and Training a Blue Lacy

3. Avoid leaving them alone outdoors. If your pooch is confined and unsupervised for longer periods of time, that will only lead to territorial behavior and allow for boredom to swoop in, both of which are usually followed with long and loud periods of barking.

If neither of these seems to do the trick, maybe you can start teaching him new words. Teaching him "Speak" and "Quit" may help you put a stop to their excessive barking:

1. First, you need to teach your pup that "Speak" means start barking. To begin this, simulate a visitor. Knock on the door or ring the bell. Make sure your pocket is filled with doggy treats.
2. The second your pup starts barking say *"Speak"* in a firm tone.
3. Praise and reward them immediately.
4. Do this for a couple of days, until your puppy learns what speak means.
5. Once your pup starts barking when you give them the speak command, it is time to teach them to be quiet. Instruct your pup to *"Speak."*
6. Once it starts barking, say *"Quiet"* in a firm tone.
7. Wait for your pup to stop barking. If needed, say *"Quiet"* again.
8. It may take a while for your pup to stop barking, and that's okay. The second it stops, praise them like crazy and give it a treat.

Chapter Five: Raising and Training a Blue Lacy

9. Respond for as long as it takes for your pooch to learn that quiet means stop barking.

Once your pup learns that, you can use this command to shush them whenever their barking starts getting just a bit too much.

Not Accepting Biting

In the first couple of weeks, biting is a normal daily hassle. But while soft mouthing is okay when your pup is playing with you, for some people, it can be a scary, if not a traumatic experience. It is extremely important for you to teach your puppy that their razor-sharp teeth are not made for the human skin while it is still a young pup in order for them to learn right from the start what it cannot play bite with. Not to mention this may prevent future injuries and even save you from a big fat lawsuit.

This training technique will discourage your pup from biting your skin as a part of its games:

1. Place one of your hands in your pup's mouth and shake it gently until it realizes you want to play.

2. Play with your pup for a while. As long as it is soft-mouthing you and doesn't apply pressure, let them have fun. The second you feel their teeth piercing a bit sharper, say *"Ouch"* or another negative word, take your hand out, and stop playing with them.

Chapter Five: Raising and Training a Blue Lacy

3. Step aside, look away, and do not interact with them for about 30 seconds. Do this for about 5-6 times a day.

4. If your pup doesn't let go of your hand the second you say "Ouch," leave the room immediately and do not let your pup see you for a couple of minutes.

5. When your pup finally realizes that ouch means it is time to let go of the hand, you can start teaching them they shouldn't play bite with humans under any circumstances.

6. It may take a while for you to get your pup to realize that it shouldn't play bite at all, but you should be patient. To start, simply play with your dog and keep your hand close to its mouth, however, do not place it inside.

7. Wait until your pup starts biting. The second it touches your skin with its teeth, even if it is super gently, say *"Bad Boy/Girl"* or another similar word, get up, and stop interacting with them for a couple of minutes.

8. Do this every time their teeth meets your skin. This way they will eventually learn biting is unacceptable.

Getting Chewing Under Control

You cannot exactly train your pup not to chew on things, and you should not even try. Chewing is not only a

Chapter Five: Raising and Training a Blue Lacy

natural instinct and an interesting way to spend their time, but it also contributes to their physical and mental health. By chewing, your pup supports the flow of antibacterial saliva and keeps his gums and teeth stay healthy and strong. That is why appropriate chew toys can jumpstart the healthy development of puppy's permanent teeth and make the whole process a lot less painful.

However, just because it is supposed to chew on things doesn't mean that your new sofa should be all chewed-up. Besides providing rubber toys, appropriate ropes, and marrow bones, there are also some other tricks that can help your pooch keep his teeth away from your possessions:

- Allow plenty of exercise. Most dogs start a chewing contest when they are bored or when they have a fair amount of extra energy they have to channel somewhere. If you don't want your couch to be that place, make sure to take your puppy on longer walks in order to knock down their urge to chew on things inside the house.
- Use taste deterrents. Taste deterrents are nasty-tasting liquids sold in spray bottles that you can use to discourage the pup from chewing on things. You can find them in most pet stores, and they are pretty cost-effective as your pup will not like the idea of chewing on something that tastes awful. These deterrents usually have no scent at all, so you shouldn't worry about having an unpleasant smell spreading inside your house. Bitter apple is a great choice for a taste deterrent.

Chapter Five: Raising and Training a Blue Lacy

When you notice them chewing on something inappropriate, simply grab the spray bottle and spray that object immediately, and let them notice you. After doing so, offer them a safe toy they can chew on to encourage appropriate behavior.

- Play a "No" and "Good Boy/Girl" game. Lay out several objects on the floor, among which you will place a couple of chew toys. Wait for them to grab an object. If it is an appropriate chewable, say "Good Boy/Girl." If not, say "No" to let your puppy know it should let go of the object.
- Praise them. In many cases, puppies are encouraged to chew on their toys when they are encouraged to do so. Whenever you see them chewing on their toys, praise them to mark the good behavior, and then give them a treat as a reward.

Stopping the Digging Frenzy

If those muddy paws freak you out, relax. You need to learn to accept this behavior as a part of the normal canine instinct. But just because it is natural, it doesn't mean that it is okay for your pup to be passing their time turning your backyard into a construction site. Whether your puppy is fussy, stressed, or just bored, you will need to find a way to make them learn that digging whenever and wherever he feels like it is not acceptable.

Although just like chewing, you cannot exactly train them not to dig. However, there are a few tricks you can do

Chapter Five: Raising and Training a Blue Lacy

that will discourage this action. The very first thing is to offer a digging spot for your puppy:

1. Pick an area in your backyard your puppy can use for digging. Make sure to mark the territory so it's easy to distinguish where it's ok to dig and where it's not. If you live in an apartment, you can provide a sandbox for digging in your bathroom from time to time, or you can even do this with a certain spot in the nearest park.
2. Bring toys to that spot, or even better, bury treats there to encourage your pup to be digging there.
3. Take your pup to that spot on a daily basis and encourage them to dig by instructing her *"Go Dig"* or another command by your choice.
4. When you catch your puppy in the act of digging someplace else, correct with a firm *"No."*

You can also give some other tricks a try:

- Dogs really dislike the citrus scent. Putting lemon or orange peels in the holes will most likely discourage your pooch from digging there.
- To help your pup learn that digging in certain areas in your yard is not acceptable, you can install some sensors such as sprinkles there.
- Do not spray your pooch with a hose when you catch them in the act. This is a common correction method many dog owners use; however, this is not only cruel, but it will also make him dig even more if it gets all fussy. Instead, you can try burying some of

Chapter Five: Raising and Training a Blue Lacy

its own feces. Dogs usually hate the smell and taste of their own feces, so give this a try if nothing else helps.
- Many dogs dig excessively when they are left alone. If that is the case, see if you can leave your pup indoors when leaving the house for a couple of hours.

Discouraging the Jumper

Dogs are social animals. It is in their nature to seek and give attention, as well as to show excitement and lavish us with love when we enter the door. Isn't that one of the main reasons why most people adopt puppies in the first place? Having a small pup jumping up every time he lays eyes on you is cute, but if this behavior is left unchecked, this can easily turn into a 60-pound force trying to knock you over. And that is something you will begin to dread.

Jumping up is one of those behaviors dog owners love to hate. Why? Because they usually start as a cute thing the pup gets rewards for, and then quickly turn into something that can cause an injury to both the dog and the owner.

So, what am I trying to say here? Never encourage a pup that is jumping up by rewarding the behavior. And I am not only talking about a reward in the form of a tasty treat. When a pup is jumping up, the reward it is seeking your attention. Rob it from that and they will soon stop performing the action that does not elicit the favorable outcome.

Chapter Five: Raising and Training a Blue Lacy

Turning Away from the Jump

When your pup jumps, the best response is to simply turn away from it. It may be heartbreaking not to give your pup attention when it is so excited to see you, but this is the most effective way to teach him to control their emotions, and believe me, once it grows into an adult dog, this trick you're teaching them now will be greatly appreciated.

Bring your hands to your chest and avoid eye contact. Once your pup sees that it gets no response, it will soon settle down. Once it is four-on-the-floor, praise them for being calm and reward them with your attention now.

Use Commands

If your pup has already mastered the "Sit" command, you can use this to get it to settle down. Again, as soon as it is on the floor, praise and reward immediately.

Go Out the Door

When you enter your door and you see your pup all excited and jumping up, simply open the door, step aside, and then close the door. Wait for your pup to calm down before going back inside. If your pooch starts jumping up again, repeat this process. Now, this may take a while, but don't lose faith. Your pup will soon pick up that you will not go through unless it greets you in a calm way. Once it does that, praise

Chapter Five: Raising and Training a Blue Lacy

them like crazy and reward them with your attention. Or a smelly treat. No dog has ever refused that.

House Training

House training is a big and demanding task and it is completely up to you how you train your dog to do his things outside the house and teach them the proper manners. It will take approximately four to six months to house train your dog, but the time frame can alter depending on their size, age, and mental acumen to learn things. Some dogs may take no time in mastering the toilet training, whereas some dogs may take up to a whole year in learning this.

Observe the Signs

You can undoubtedly get the hint as to when you dog wants to leak out as he will start looking around anxiously and walk in circles and begin to sniff around in cornered places of the house, looking for a suitable place and that is their strong signal to you so you may catch the signals outside immediately. You should patiently take your dog to the toilet and then wait for him outside with maintained patience as they may take longer than usual. It is because when outdoors, the dog gets excited and starts playing around before relieving himself. You should not hurry them and rather than let them go until they are all ready.

Chapter Five: Raising and Training a Blue Lacy

Some Basic Rules to Follow

Take your puppy to the toilet area soon after he wakes up and after he is done eating or drinking so that it can become a permanent habit for them to follow. Do allocate a fix toilet area as it will help the dog to recognize the place easily when he starts going out himself. Be punctual in rewarding them or showering them with praises once they go to pee at the right place so that it remains fresh in their minds. Make sure that you give them plenty of chances to go to the toilet every two hours. Avoid punishing your puppy during this training process as it might ruin every accomplished thing. Toilet training is a slow process so think of your puppy as a toddler and remember that he can make mistakes too. Consistency is the key to fast house training because accidents are a regular part of such training processes, but you should always stay happy and relaxed towards your dog. Being patient throughout can be a difficult thing to carry out because cleaning and wiping the house regularly can threaten this virtue. It is normal that they take longer time in getting used to the toilet habits.

When taking in view the toilet training habits, you would necessarily want your dog to clearly differentiate between the play area of your garden and the outdoor toilet area. You can help them understand this difference by marking the area with a fence or a chip wood. This toilet area will look different and of course smell different from the rest of the place, and your dog would quickly grasp the difference.

Chapter Five: Raising and Training a Blue Lacy

Most puppies prefer green and ground places as they have a particular scent which they can catch easily and can find the toilet place, in contrast to hard surfaces such as concrete areas. It is important to regularly clean their toilet to encourage them to go back when required. Believe it or not, but animals are very meticulous about the cleanliness of the places where they relieve themselves. Left over mess in the toilet area can put them off and this may lead them to look to other places for the purpose and disrupt the training progress.

Routine is a Must

Take your puppy to the allotted toilet on regular bases to let them use it and then keep in mind to reward them afterwards so they associate this act to good behavior as well. If they sniff around and do not do anything, be patient with them because you might have to give them some time. However, if they still resist, bring them inside and observe them for five minutes. Take them out immediately if you sense any warning sign from them of needing to use the toilet.

It is a good idea to introduce a few accompanying words while toilet training a dog such as 'busy' or 'hurry' when they are going to the toilet so that they may understand these words when at a new place. Connecting command words with actions can help the dogs to recall the terms whenever required.

Chapter Five: Raising and Training a Blue Lacy

Take them out of the toilet area after they are done with it and play with them for a while so that they can realize the change, then bring them back.

As part of house training a puppy, you need to take them out to toilet early in the morning and every time they get to eat or drink something. Moreover, keep it in mind to appreciate them each time they get it right.

Getting your dog out in time may be hard in case there is no garden, or you are living in an apartment. Therefore, it is vital to identify the signs your puppy is giving to inform you that they need to pee. You can use your family's support in this case.

Little Things to Keep in Mind

Adjusting and arranging little things can save you from the real trouble in the future training. If you are living in an apartment, then it is a better option to make use of baby gates as puppies enjoy relieving themselves far away from where they spend most of their time. These small barriers can bound them to a specific area where they are staying and when it would be the time for toilet training, they would wait eagerly for their handlers to make them move to some far place to pee or poop, which means that the frequency of

Chapter Five: Raising and Training a Blue Lacy

accidents would get considerably reduced as they would not roam around on their own.

It is beneficial if you set a timer to take your dog out after every two or three hours. It is necessary because often we become so engrossed in our other chores that we lose the track of time which can impede the normal routine of your dog's training, making him more vulnerable to accidents.

For a short term, puppy training pads can come in handy, but this is not helpful in the long run as it might confuse the dogs and significantly delay the overall training period. Sometimes, when you are left with no other option than using the puppy pads, then it is most suited if you keep the pads closer to the door so they may link it with the signal of going out to use the toilet.

Dealing with Accidents

Accidents in the house are bound to occur during the initial training days, but if your puppy uses the indoor toilet it is imperative to relax and tell yourself that its part of learning, just like you would deal with a child.

In case you find a wet patch, just wipe it up without creating a fuss about it and do this in absence of your puppy as you do not want him to feel embarrassed and demotivated.

Chapter Five: Raising and Training a Blue Lacy

Never get irritated or annoyed in front of them, if it happens, as it is not justified to reprimand them for something that is not in their control. If you see them peeing, just bring them out to the toilet area to finish, then clean the floor with disinfectant and use air freshener so there is no bad odor and your dog cannot take it as a toilet area.

Crate Training

If you do not have a backyard or a garden, then it is better to go with this kind of training method. Also, this method comes in handy at nighttime. It is better to choose crate training from all the other house-training methods, because the dogs are already aware of this training method. When the puppies are living with their mums, they are taught not to wet their sleeping place, and so by employing the crate, we just continue with what their mums have already trained them.

It is good to keep the puppies in the crate for only a short span of time, because if kept longer then it can make them uncomfortable.

Combine toilet training with sleep training

If you consider it likely, it is much healthier to amalgamate puppy toilet training with crate and sleep training as your pet will still require going out at night in these early weeks. Your puppy's toilet usage at night might

Chapter Five: Raising and Training a Blue Lacy

get reduced if you use crate training as the puppy will be less likely to wet its sleeping place.

A large puppy should just need 1-2 further visits at night. Smaller breeds are expected to go out more frequently at nighttime until they age. When bringing them out at night, attempt not to give your puppy extra devotion instead keep the process straightforward and monotonous before bringing them back to bed. You should not urge them to play at this time as they might not want to sleep afterwards.

Just Keep Going

If you are consistent in using any method for the toilet training of your dog, then he will eventually learn to use the outdoor toilet. You may face frequent failures, which are a very natural part of training so try not to panic and just increase your dog's outdoor trips until he gets well-aware of his routine and follows it properly. Gradually, your dog will get that he must pee outside the house, and you will also be able to readily catch their body signals.

Training Your Dog for Public Situations

At this point in the book, you should have a direction where you want to take the training for your dog. The next step is to properly train your dog for outside situations as you will likely be taking your dog for lots of walks and visits to the dog park. Training your dog for public situations is a

Chapter Five: Raising and Training a Blue Lacy

combination of learning the right technique for walking your dog and obedience training. Obedience training is often utilized during these situations as your dog may get overly excited when they see other dogs or friendly people. You may need to use certain commands to control their behavior to prevent any accidents. Let's first take a look at how to properly walk your dog.

How to Walk Your Dog

One of the hardest parts about managing your dog's behavior outside of your home is while you are walking him/her on a leash. This takes up almost 99% of the time you are outside with your dog. Learning the proper walking techniques will make your life easier and your dog happier. Let's take a look at 10 different walking tips that you should follow to make the walks with your dog more enjoyable and manageable.

1. If your dog pulls on your leash, use a front clip harness.

Many dogs that are excited tend to constantly pull on their leashes. Certain dog collars and leashes actually make it easy for dogs to pull more and promotes more pulling during a walk. Getting a front clip harness is one of the best investments you can make when it comes to walking your dog. When you are shopping for this leash, check the front of the dog harness to see if there is a clip at the front of the harness. Although having a front clip harness won't solve all

Chapter Five: Raising and Training a Blue Lacy

your problems, it certainly makes it harder for your dog to get into the habit of pulling.

2. Allow your dog to sniff his/her surroundings.

Although to you, walking your dog may be a necessity to let your dog relieve him/herself while giving him/her exercise. However, to your dog, the walks are the only time during the day that they can go out and explore. Give your dog some extra time and let them explore their surroundings and sniff around. This will help them get socialized better to the environment they're in. If you don't want to stop every 10 seconds to let your dog sniff around, choose areas that you deem are safe and appropriate and allow your dog to sniff around and explore. All the smells that your dog is experiencing provide them with information and stimulation. It is your dog's way to keep track of everything that's going on in your neighborhood. Also, sniffing takes energy; you'd be surprised at how much more energy is burned if you allow your dog to sniff his/her environment.

3. Don't use retractable leashes when walking your dog.

A rule of thumb for most experienced dog owners is to avoid using retractable leashes on walks. Retractable leashes cause numerous hazards compared to your traditional leashes. The problem with retractable leashes is that the length of the leash itself makes it hard for you to control your dog, especially if you are walking in busy areas. Most dogs can easily run into the street with retractable leashes as they are not easy to reel in. Those locks that are in retractable

Chapter Five: Raising and Training a Blue Lacy

leashes have also been known to disengage if pulled on with enough pressure. Retractable leashes have also been known to injure both dogs and humans. The next time you go shopping for a new leash, avoid retractable leashes, and stick with front clip harnesses.

4. Always clean up after your dog.

When walking your dog, always remember to pick up your dog's poop. This simple action is much more than just being a good neighbor. Dog poop that is left in public causes many health concerns to both humans and dogs. Dog poop can contain dangerous organisms like E. coli and salmonella. This can easily be spread to other animals in your area. Make sure you are always stocked up on poop bags; they are cheap and can be bought in any pet store or even convenience store. Opt for the biodegradable ones if possible!

5. Bring plenty of water during your walks.

If it is summer or you are living in a warm climate, make sure you bring enough water for your dog. Dogs have difficulty regulating their temperature compared to humans. It is actually very easy for dogs to overheat. They can become dehydrated quite easily if they go without water for a while. Buy a collapsible water bottle and give your dog water every 30 minutes or so.

6. Make sure your dog has an ID tag.

Chapter Five: Raising and Training a Blue Lacy

Every time you and your dog leave your home, make sure they are wearing a form of identification. Accidents happen and dogs can accidentally run away from their owners during walks. In order to be able to track your dog down afterward, make sure they are microchipped so if anyone finds them, they can contact you through the information on the microchip. Having a dog tag with your dog's information and your contact information will ensure that whoever finds your dog can contact you in a timely manner.

7. Be careful of hot pavements during the summertime.

Depending on where you live, summers may get hot enough where the pavement can literally burn your skin. Before you take your dog out on a walk on pavement, place your hand on the ground to see how hot it is. Hold your hand there for at least 5 seconds; if the pavement feels too hot, then it is definitely too hot for your dog's paws. Instead, opt for a walk in the grass or in the woods. If your dog is tolerant of it, you can get your dog some booties/shoes to protect their paws.

8. Bring dog treats to keep your dog focused.

Everywhere that you go to walk, your dog will be filled with numerous distractions. Make sure you bring plenty of treats for you in order to practice some obedience training and positive reinforcement when they complete a desired command or behavior. For instance, if your dog is distracted and wanting to chase after a squirrel, get his/her attention by

Chapter Five: Raising and Training a Blue Lacy

telling her to sit/stay and provide him/her with a treat once it's achieved!

9. Ask owners before approaching their dog.

Although most dogs are pleasant around other dogs, this is not always 100% the case. Don't take any risks and ask the dog's owner that your dog wants to approach if they're okay with it. Most owners know whether their dog is good with other dogs or not. Check with them before allowing an interaction so no accidents happen!

10. Wear reflective gear if walking at night.

Just like your neighborhood runners, make sure you and your dog are wearing some sort of reflective gear if you're taking him/her out at night. Some nights can be extremely poor for visibility; don't take any risks and make sure that you are clearly visible by everyone else on the road.

Using Obedience Training During Walks

Obedience training is crucial when walking your dog in public. Simple commands such as "sit" and "stay" can change a situation dramatically. Make sure your dog has basic obedience training and is able to listen to commands outside of your home before taking him/her out for long walks or to dog parks. Let's do a quick review of what obedience training is.

Chapter Five: Raising and Training a Blue Lacy

The idea behind obedience training is to train your dog into 100% obedience using commands. This is a more advanced level of training, and your dog should already have basic knowledge of behavioral training. The main difference between behavioral training and obedience training is that you don't need a reason or specific behavior to initiate a command. For example, in behavioral training if your dog was jumping at a guest, you would use the command 'sit' to prevent that bad action. In obedience training, you are giving your dog commands regardless of the circumstance and they will listen to you 100%.

Most puppies or younger dogs will go through beginner level obedience training, which is simply by learning the common commands. Once your dog has the basics down, they should be able to learn more difficult and advanced level commands. Obedience training is required for your dog to participate in even more advanced levels of training such as agility training or vocational training. During obedience training, your dog will learn commands via verbal cues and non-verbal cues like hand gestures.

As we learned earlier, be sure to have trained your dog to be able to utilize these five commands when you are out in public:

- "Sit": Your dog will be in a sitting position where his/her front paws are in front of them, and their buttocks are touching the floor.

- "Down": Your dog is in a position where he/she is lying down. His/her front feet, legs, and chest are touching the ground.

Chapter Five: Raising and Training a Blue Lacy

- "Come": Your dog will come to you.

- "Stay": Your dog will stay still in the same position as to where you made that command.

- "Heel": Your dog's head will be parallel to your legs when you guys are walking. If he/she is in front of you, he/she will come back to your side

Chapter Five: Raising and Training a Blue Lacy

Chapter Six: Grooming Your Blue Lacy

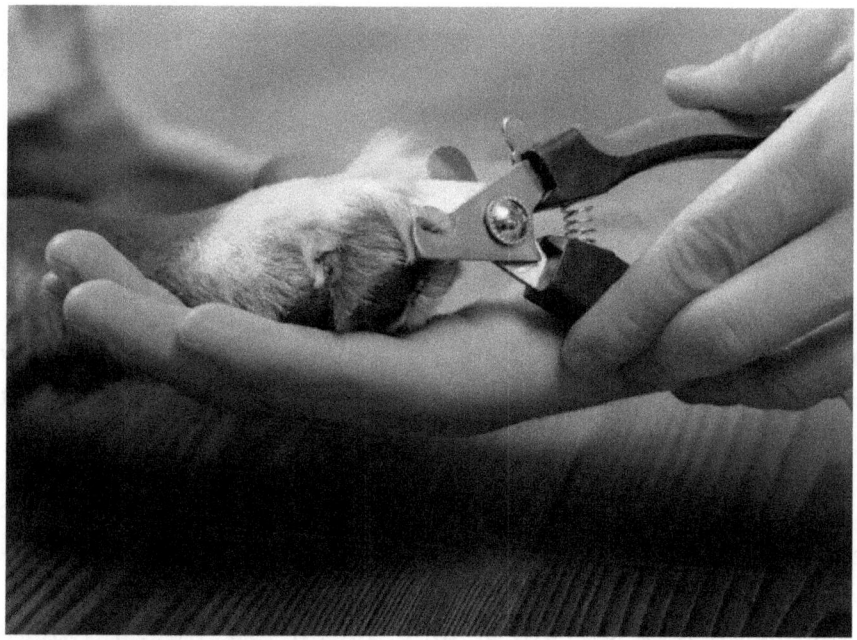

Grooming a Blue Lacy is easy. This breed has a tight, short coat, which does not carry burs, and also does not tangle to form nasty mats. Your Blue Lacy should always have a good coat, with very little shedding. Proper grooming will help to keep your Blue Lacy looking and feeling his best. Regular grooming also helps to prevent health problems related to poor hygiene.

Grooming and Parasites

Before we get into the actual grooming and bathing, it is worth mentioning parasites that you may encounter whilst grooming. Fleas, ticks and mites are the most likely culprits

Chapter Six: Grooming Your Blue Lacy

you will encounter. Fortunately, as the coat of your Blue Lacy is relatively short, fleas in particular are not as problematic as longer, double coated dogs. Fleas prefer to bury and hide themselves in a relatively thick coat. They are therefore bound to feel more exposed, vulnerable and less safe on a thin, less dense coat. They will also be much easier to pick out with fine toothed flea combs.

The added problem with fleas, is that they can also set up home in the dogs bedding or the furnishings of your home. It is therefore necessary to not only treat the dog, but their bedding and your furnishings. If you ever get a particularly bad infestation, it may be necessary to call in professional pest controllers.

It is up to you what remedies you use on your dog. So called 'spot on' treatments are commonly recommended by vets. They do work, but a lot of dog owners, who are more organically inclined, are against the idea of applying these because of a potential toxic effect to the dog. It is not for me to comment about the long-term effect of any such toxins to the future health of the dog.

If you use a 'spot on' treatment, they are generally affective for one or two months depending on the product. It is also worth bearing in mind that although there are shampoos that claim, to be effective against fleas, I would never rely on these as a regular flea treatment remedy. As we have stated above, regular bathing with shampoos is not recommended. By all means use a shampoo that offers flea treatment, but only for when you bathe your dog.

Chapter Six: Grooming Your Blue Lacy

Generally, insecticides available from either your vet or pet shop will be needed to deal with ticks and mites. Fleas seem to be a common problem for most geographical areas, but tics are not a problem for all. So again, not everyone will have a problem with all parasites.

Tools and Methods

Some dogs do not react well to grooming because they do not like being held still. Because grooming is so important however, you should get your puppy used to grooming from an early age. Brush your puppy for a few seconds at a time several times a day until he no longer seems bothered by it. Then you can cut back to one longer brushing session each day and then as I said, perhaps once per week will be all that is needed. You should also frequently touch your puppy's paws and ears so that once you start trimming his nails and cleaning his ears he will be used to this kind of handling.

When grooming, always be gentle and brush or comb, with slow careful strokes. The last thing you want is for your dog to start shaking and be left traumatized, or the very least, disliking the experience. Blue Lacys are generally a clean breed so they may not require a lot of bathing.

Again, the adult Blue Lacy requires a weekly brush at the very least to keep their coat in good condition and prevent hair around the house. Daily grooming with a fine bristle brush is recommended by some owners and particularly when they shed usually around spring and then winter time. You will hear different stories from different owners as far as

Chapter Six: Grooming Your Blue Lacy

hair shedding. Some report a high frequency and some hardly any at all.

Be careful not to use grooming brushes/rakes more suitable for thick double coated dogs. Remember the Blue Lacy has a relatively thin coat. A brush that is too harsh will hurt your Blue Lacy's delicate skin. This will also make the grooming experience unpleasant and at worse traumatic.

A massage with a rubber hound glove should follow, and this keeps the Blue Lacy's coat smooth and his skin healthy. Your Blue Lacy puppy should become accustomed to being groomed every day if needed. Some Blue Lacys may struggle in the beginning, but most Blue Lacys learn to enjoy the bonding and close contact.

I would suggest preceding grooming with the following:

1. It is entirely up to you, but I prefer to regularly hand rub the coat and skin, first of all. This serves two purposes, firstly you are effectively massaging your dog as well as removing any dead loose hair and skin. Secondly, it allows you to check your Blue Lacy for any lumps, bumps or sensitive skin parts that may require attention. Remember to take your Blue Lacy to the veterinarian if you notice any unusual lumps or skin irritations.

2. This is then followed with a good brushing, preferably with a bristle brush that isn't too stiff. In order to remove as much dead skin and hair, do this against the lay of the coat. This effectively roughs up the coat, but is a lot more thorough than simply brushing with the lay.

Chapter Six: Grooming Your Blue Lacy

3. You can finish by brushing back the coat, with the lay, using the bristle brush. Some people prefer to use hound gloves if you can get one, or a rubber curry comb.

4. Also check for any long hairs that appear around the legs or muzzle. It is best to trim these with a pair of blunt ended scissors, to avoid accidentally stabbing your dog as you trim.

Rubber Curry Comb: The curry comb fits into your palm and contains flexible rubber nibs. It works by loosening your Blue Lacy's undercoat, and brings all the grime to the surface of your Blue Lacy t's coat.

Bathing your Blue Lacy

On occasion it may be necessary to bathe your Blue Lacy, in particular if whilst outdoors he gets muddy. As a matter of routine, you could always use an old towel to dry your dog's legs and feet, on damp, wet outings. You will usually find that this sufficiently dries and cleans any soiled areas.

Organic or Natural Shampoo: Blue Lacys do best with an organic or natural, chemical free shampoo. Since they are prone to skin sensitivities, dry skin, or flaky skin. Because of this it is best not to wash your Blue Lacy very often and certainly not every week. If you have to wash mud from their legs, feet or coat, please do this with warm water, but no shampoo. You can then either towel dry and or use a hair drier to ensure your do does not get chilled.

Chapter Six: Grooming Your Blue Lacy

Avoid bathing your dog on a regular basis as this strips the skin and coat of natural healthy oils. Remember that your Blue Lacy's skin has a pH of 7.5, while humans have a pH of 5.5. That said, never use human shampoo on your Blue Lacy. This will lead to scaling and skin irritation. There are numerous dog shampoos available for various canine skin problems.

Remember also that Blue Lacys dislike being cold, or generally getting wet. Be sure therefore to always use warm water, but not too warm and never hot. Your Blue Lacy needs to have a positive experience with water when being bathed.

Don't forget that your dog relies on natural oils to keep the skin soft, healthy and free from drying out. The oil also has the benefit of protecting the coat and retaining its water resistance. It is tempting to consider how grubby and uncomfortable us humans feel when we don't bathe regularly. However, you cannot take that same viewpoint where your dog is concerned.

Some Blue Lacy owners advocate rubbing olive oil into the coat prior to bathing. This is especially useful if the dog has an obvious skin problem. This is fine, but I would further add that it is probably a good idea to do this after wards as well, until he replenishes his natural oils once more. I wouldn't advise using too much though, as you do not wish to have oil all over your furnishings. A few drops that you brush into the coat after he is dry, is probably all you need. Or if you are aware of any sensitive areas, then perhaps apply a little oil to those parts only.

Chapter Six: Grooming Your Blue Lacy

To bathe your Blue Lacy at home, follow the steps outlined below:

1. Give your Blue Lacy a good brushing before you bathe him to get rid of accumulated loose hair.
2. Fill your bathtub with a few inches of lukewarm water. You may also want to put down a rubber bath mat so your dog doesn't slip in the tub.
3. Place your Blue Lacy in the tub and wet down his fur with a handheld hose or by pouring water over him.
4. Avoid getting your Blue Lacy's eyes and ears wet when you bathe him. Wet ears are a breeding ground for bacteria that could cause an ear infection.
5. Apply a small amount of mild dog-friendly shampoo to your Blue Lacy's back and gently work it into a lather along his neck, back, chest and legs.
6. Rinse the soap thoroughly out of your Blue Lacy s coat and use a damp washcloth to clean his face.
7. Some professional groomers at this stage advise that whilst the dog is still wet, to give a brisk rub with a hound glove or rubber grooming glove to remove excess hair
8. Use a large fluffy towel to towel-dry your Blue Lacy, getting as much water out of his coat as possible. If it is warm you can let him air-dry the rest of the way.

If your Blue Lacy seems to be cold you can use a hair-dryer on the low heat setting to dry him the rest of the way.

You can bathe your Blue Lacy if he gets dirty, but you should avoid bathing him when it is not necessary. Over-bathing a dog can dry out his skin and lead to skin problems.

Chapter Six: Grooming Your Blue Lacy

In some cases you may be able to brush dried dirt and debris out of your Blue Lacy's coat instead of bathing him.

Trimming your dog's nails

Puppy Nail Clippers

The best clippers to use on a Blue Lacy puppy will be cat nail clippers. These are made especially for thin, small nails. As your Blue Lacy grows older, you'll learn to alternate and use the regular dog nail clipper. These cut thicker adult canine nails. When buying nail clippers, pick up some styptic powder, which can be used on any bleeding caused from a too-closely clipped nail. It also works as an antiseptic. Obviously try not to nick the quick when cutting your Blue Lacy's nails.

Trimming your Blue Lacy's nails can be challenging because you need to be very careful. A dog's nail contains a quick; the vessel that brings blood to the nail. If you cut the nail too short you will cut the quick. This not only causes your dog pain, but it can bleed profusely as well. When you trim your Blue Lacy's nails you should only cut the very tip to remove the point. Depending on what colour your dog's nails are, you may be able to see the quick and use it as a trimming guide.

It is generally recommended that you trim your Blue Lacy's nails every two weeks. If you do it this often then you will only need to clip the slightest amount off the nail each time. This will reduce the risk of cutting the quick. Before you

Chapter Six: Grooming Your Blue Lacy

trim your Blue Lacy's nails for the first time you should consider having a veterinarian or a professional groomer show you how. You also need to be sure you are using real dog nail clippers for the job. Please also be aware that you shouldn't attempt to clip your dog's nails routinely every two weeks, just for the sake of it, as he may not need it. You should notice that if your dog walks on pavements or your concrete yard, he will to a certain extent be filing them down anyway.

Cleaning your dog's ears

Your dog's risk of ear infection increases significantly if you get the ears wet, such as during a bath.

Cleaning your dog's ears is not difficult, but you do need the right supplies. Gear up with a bottle of dog-friendly ear cleaning solution, preferably recommended by your vet, and a few clean cotton balls.

1. Gently hold your dog's ear and squeeze a few drops of the cleaning solution into the ear canal.
2. Massage the ear canal, around the base of the dog's ear, to spread the solution then use the cotton balls to wipe it away.
3. Be careful not to put your fingers or the cotton ball too far into your dog's ear or you could damage his ear drum.

Please also avoid cleaning with cotton buds as again they could cause internal damage. The frequency with which you

Chapter Six: Grooming Your Blue Lacy

clean your Blue Lacy's ears will vary but you should aim for once every week or two.

Brushing your Blue Lacy's teeth

The idea of brushing your dog's teeth may sound strange but dental health is just as important for your dog as it is for you. In fact, periodontitis (gum disease) is five times more common in dogs than in humans. Gum disease is incredibly serious but it often goes unnoticed by pet parents, especially since many people think that dogs are supposed to have bad breath. Bad breath, or halitosis, is one of the most common signs of gum disease and could be indicative of a tooth abscess. Once again, please note that dogs regularly chewing on suitable raw meaty bones have relatively odorless breath. If you suspect an abscess, or anything un-toward, seek a veterinary examination as soon as possible.

To brush your Blue Lacy's teeth, follow the steps below:

1. Select a soft-bristle toothbrush to use. Most pet stores stock special toothbrushes for dogs.
2. Choose a toothpaste that is specifically made for dogs, never human tooth paste. They come in a variety of flavors, so select one your Blue Lacy will like. He will probably like them all. Again, never use the tooth paste you use. These contain chemicals that can be harmful to dogs.
3. Get your dog used to having his teeth handled by gently placing your finger in his mouth against his

Chapter Six: Grooming Your Blue Lacy

teeth. Carefully manipulate his lips so he gets used to the feeling.
4. If you find he doesn't particularly like this, try dipping your finger in peanut butter or chicken broth so your dog learns to like the treatment.
5. When you are ready to brush, place one hand over your dog's mouth and gently pull back his lips.
6. Apply a small amount of toothpaste to the brush and rub it gently over a few of his teeth.
7. After a few seconds, stop brushing and give your Blue Lacy a treat for good behavior.
8. Slowly increase the length of your brushing sessions over a few days until your dog lets you brush all of his teeth in one session.

In addition to brushing your Blue Lacy's teeth at home you should also make sure he gets a dental check-up from the vet every 6 months.

Chapter Six: Grooming Your Blue Lacy

Chapter Seven: Vet Care for Your Blue Lacy

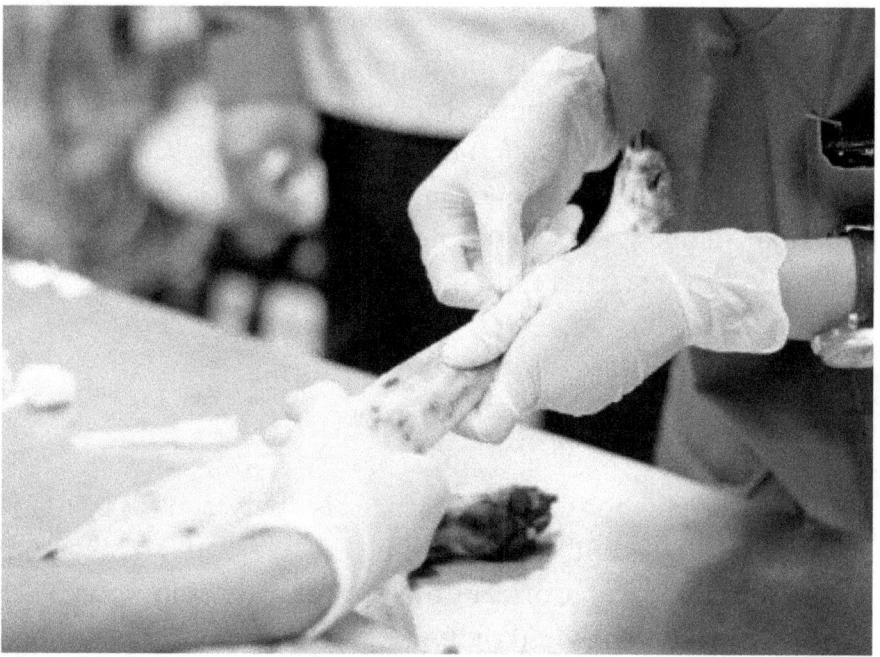

Common Illnesses and Injuries

Even when you take the very best care of your Blue Lacy that you can, he will get sick or hurt at some point. Some common illnesses and injuries can be taken care of with home care, while others require a trip to the vet. As a responsible pet owner, it's important for you to be aware of common problems that may develop and to know what to do about them. A good relationship with your veterinarian is also very important.

Chapter Seven: Vet Care for Your Blue Lacy

What's Normal?

In order for you to judge whether your Blue Lacy is ill, you need to have some sense of what normal is. If you observe your Blue Lacy carefully on a daily basis, you'll be able to identify when something is "off." Sometimes it's just a feeling you have. Listen to it. If the problem doesn't seem serious enough to involve the veterinarian, make a note of it in your calendar. This way, if symptoms do worsen, you'll know when you first started noticing that something was up.

Body Temperature

Normal body temperature is between 100.5 and 102.5°F for dogs, with 101.3°F being the average. To take your dog's temperature, lubricate the end of a thermometer with some petroleum jelly, KY Jelly, or butter, then lift his tail and insert the thermometer into his rectum until the silver end is covered. Hold it there for a minute or two. (If you're using a digital thermometer, wait for it to beep.) Make sure your dog doesn't sit down so you don't risk breaking the thermometer while it's still inside him.

If your dog's temperature is below 99°F or above 104°F, contact your veterinarian immediately, or visit the nearest emergency facility.

Chapter Seven: Vet Care for Your Blue Lacy

When should blood work be done?

Blood tests can provide a look into what's going on inside your dog. If your dog is eight or older, an annual — or even twice yearly — blood chemistry test is a good idea for early detection of disease or organ failure.

The Annual Exam

Every dog should visit the veterinarian at least once a year for a wellness checkup. At that exam, your vet will give your dog a thorough looking-over, examining his eyes, ears, teeth, skin, and coat. She'll palpate him, feeling for lumps or signs of pain. She'll also probably want a stool sample to check for worms and a blood sample for a heartworm test. This annual appointment is important for early detection of disease and for allowing your vet to see your dog when he's feeling well.

Problem Visits

In an ideal world, your Blue Lacy wouldn't need to see the vet any more often than his annual wellness appointment. But there's a real possibility that you'll need to take your Blue Lacy in because of some illness or injury. Don't be afraid to set up an appointment if you feel a problem is serious or if it is not clearing up with your home remedies.

When it comes to deciding whether to pay a visit to the vet, listen to your intuition. If it tells you that something

Chapter Seven: Vet Care for Your Blue Lacy

serious is going on, it's worth it (if only for your peace of mind) to visit or call your vet.

Relieving Blue Lacy Allergies

Allergies to food or pollens are not uncommon in Blue Lacys, or dogs in general. An allergic reaction is an immune response to something to which the body is overly sensitive. Generally, allergies in dogs manifest themselves in itchiness. Your Blue Lacy might lick his paws or scratch his ears or the back of his front legs. Allergies can also lead to red, goopy eyes or gastrointestinal problems.

Inhalant Allergies

Inhalant allergens such as grasses, pollens, mold, or dust tend to make a dog very itchy and can lead to miserable skin problems. However, it is very difficult to avoid allergens in the air. Since allergies are essentially caused by an imbalance in the immune system, there are two approaches to take: suppressing the immune system so that it won't react, or balancing the immune system.

If your Blue Lacy is suffering from allergies, don't vaccinate him. Vaccinations introduce foreign proteins into your dog's system and give an already out-of-balance immune system an unpleasant jolt. Vaccinations should be given only to healthy dogs; allergic dogs are not healthy.

Conventional therapy for severe allergies is to use corticosteroids like prednisone to suppress the immune

Chapter Seven: Vet Care for Your Blue Lacy

system. Unfortunately, long-term steroid use is hard on your dog's body and can potentially lead to serious problems. While cortisone can provide your Blue Lacy relief — which can be very important — it can also shorten his life. Another conventional approach is allergy shots, which contain small amounts of the allergen that your Blue Lacy is sensitive to. These allergens are injected into your dog, in hopes of slowly reducing his sensitivity to the allergens.

An alternative approach is to consult with a holistic vet about nutritional therapy to help balance the immune system. Other holistic modalities, like homeopathy, glandular therapy, herbs, acupressure, and acupuncture, can also be helpful. Once the immune system is balanced, it will stop overreacting to the allergens.

Food Allergies

Food allergies, which happen when a dog becomes overly sensitive to an ingredient in his diet, can lead to itchiness, inflamed ears, and gastrointestinal problems. Dogs become hypersensitive to ingredients they eat day in and day out. Grains are often a source of allergies. If your Blue Lacy develops a food allergy, you can switch diets to avoid the offending ingredient and seek to increase your dog's overall health with holistic support.

You may want to consider switching to a home-prepared diet. This will give you more control over what goes into your dog's body. Also, the fresh ingredients in the home

Chapter Seven: Vet Care for Your Blue Lacy

diet can lead to increased health, which can, in turn, reduce the allergic reaction.

Diagnosing Allergies

Food allergies are often diagnosed through an elimination diet. This means you feed your dog a very limited diet of ingredients he's never eaten before. Then you slowly add the ingredients of his old food to determine what is causing the reaction.

This type of strategy doesn't work with environmental or inhalant allergies since you don't have control over the environment the same way you do over food. But two types of tests are available to determine the allergens. One is the intradermal skin test, done under sedation, in which antigens are injected into the skin so the sites can be examined for reaction. A less invasive option is blood testing. Some veterinarians say that blood tests aren't reliable for allergies, but many holistic vets have used them with great success. They're easy to do and provide detailed results.

If your Blue Lacy has itchy skin or a poor coat, and you suspect allergies, ask your veterinarian to draw blood for a complete thyroid panel. An underactive thyroid can cause these symptoms. Your vet should run a full panel, not just a T4 test, which is an unreliable indicator on its own.

Chapter Seven: Vet Care for Your Blue Lacy

Cuts and Scrapes

If your rough-and-tumble Blue Lacy gets a few cuts or scrapes, you can treat them like you would a kid's scraped knee. Wash the area with some soap and water and apply some Neosporin or calendula ointment (a natural antibiotic available at the health food store). For deeper cuts that may need stitches, take him in to see the vet. Watch for signs of infection as the wound heals (redness, swelling, or tenderness). If you think you have an infection on your hands, call your vet.

Dealing with Foxtails

Foxtails are small grasses with brush-like spikes full of seeds. The seeds have barbed sides and sharp ends, and when they're dry (as they are in the summer and fall) they can attach themselves to your dog. If you don't remove them, they can get entangled deeper and deeper into the fur and can even go through the skin and enter the body. Foxtails can also get caught in the nose, eyes, and ears. They cause pain and discomfort for your Blue Lacy and, if they enter the body, can be dangerous and hard to detect.

If your Blue Lacy has been running through tall grass, inspect him thoroughly when he's finished and remove any foxtails or burrs that you find. If your Blue Lacy is sneezing repetitively, shaking his head or pawing at his ears, do a close inspection for foxtails. If he's squinting or licking a paw, it might be due to foxtails. If you find one that's become

Chapter Seven: Vet Care for Your Blue Lacy

imbedded, particularly if it's in the eye, ear, or nose, take him to the vet for immediate removal.

Relief from Hot Spots

Raw, weepy spots on your Blue Lacy's skin, known as hot spots, are usually caused by the Blue Lacy himself. He gets an itch from something, like an allergic reaction to a fleabite, and licks it and chews on it until it's raw. A healthy, natural way to provide him some relief and help make the hot spot go away is to make a paste from water and powdered bovine colostrum (available in powder and capsules at health food stores) and apply it directly on the hot spot. It will soothe and also help heal. Aloe gel (either from the health food store or directly from the plant) can also be soothing and healing. Clipping the fur around the hot spot can help it air out and stay dry.

Lumps and Bumps

Feeling for lumps should be part of your routine at-home examination of your Blue Lacy. Dogs can get all sorts of lumps, ranging from benign fatty lipomas to abscesses to cancerous tumors. If you find a lump on your dog, contact your veterinarian so you can get an expert's opinion. Your vet may want to remove it or aspirate it with a needle to look for cancerous cells.

It's scary to find a lump on your Blue Lacy. As he ages, they will crop up more and more often, and you'll probably

Chapter Seven: Vet Care for Your Blue Lacy

become an expert about knowing when to worry. Make sure your vet feels them, and ask her to keep a map of your Blue Lacy 's lumps and bumps in his chart, so it's easy to monitor them.

Gastrointestinal Problems

Loose, watery stools and vomiting can be caused by all sorts of things, ranging from the relatively innocuous (dietary indiscretion) to the serious (metabolic problems). Sometimes it's nothing to fret about, but if it's happening frequently, a vet visit is usually in order.

Diarrhea

If your Blue Lacy has occasional diarrhea and you can figure out a relatively harmless cause (stress or excitement or a snack of spicy food, for example), it's not something to worry about. In general, it's a good idea to let diarrhea run its course, since the body uses diarrhea to flush out toxins.

When your dog has diarrhea, withhold food for twelve to twenty-four hours, keeping water available so he doesn't become dehydrated. Then feed bland food, like boiled chicken or hamburger (with fat rinsed off after boiling), or scrambled or soft-boiled eggs accompanied by cottage cheese or white rice. Slowly ease him back to his regular food.

However, if the diarrhea occurs frequently, lasts more than two days, is bloody or black, or is accompanied by vomiting, weakness, or fever, give your vet a call. Together, you should try to find the source of the problem and address it.

Vomiting

Vomiting can also be caused by a number of factors. Something as simple as stress or drinking water too fast might make your Blue Lacy vomit. If he regurgitates his food right after eating, then tries to eat it again, he may have just eaten too fast.

If your dog vomits just once and seems to feel well otherwise, don't worry too much about it (though it's a good idea to mark it on your calendar). If your dog vomits a couple of times but is otherwise healthy, withhold food for twelve hours, then feed him a small amount of bland food.

If your Blue Lacy is uncomfortable and tries to vomit but is unable to do so, feel his belly. If it's hard or distended at all, he may be bloating. Bloat is a medical emergency in which the stomach fills with air or gas and twists. If you think your Blue Lacy might be bloating, rush him to the emergency vet.

If your dog is vomiting violently and frequently, or if the vomit smells like feces or contains blood, contact your veterinarian. If the vomiting is accompanied by severe diarrhea, a vet visit is also in order.

Chapter Seven: Vet Care for Your Blue Lacy

Lack of Appetite

If your Blue Lacy normally scarfs down everything you put in front of him, lack of appetite can be an important indicator that something is up. Not wanting to eat is a sign of a number of illnesses, including Addison's disease and cancer. It can also be a sign of poor dental health or infectious disease. Of course, it can also just be a message that your Blue Lacy doesn't like what you're feeding him! If your Blue Lacy refuses to eat, first try offering him something else. If he won't eat anything and he seems to be feeling poorly, take him to the vet.

Ear Infections

Thanks to their dogs' medium and thin ears, most Blue Lacy owners are very familiar with ear infections. They're not hard to detect. You might notice your Blue Lacy shaking his head a lot or scratching his ears. When you smell the ears during your regular at-home exam, they might stink. If the infection is quite bad, your Blue Lacy might cry out or flinch when you try to handle his ears.

Treating Ear Infections

If your Blue Lacy has an infection, your veterinarian might prescribe antibiotics to fight it. If the infection is particularly severe, your Blue Lacy may need to be anesthetized so that the ears can be flushed out.

Chapter Seven: Vet Care for Your Blue Lacy

One product that can help clear up ear infections without antibiotics or steroids is called Zymox Otic, made by Pet King Brands, Inc. It uses four types of enzymes to fight bacterial, viral, and fungal infections. It works quickly and painlessly and comes with or without hydrocortisone, which can help reduce pain and inflammation. Ask your veterinarian if she can order some if she doesn't already have it.

Antibiotics may sometimes be necessary, but if your Blue Lacy has recurrent infections, you'll need to do more than give your dog course after course of antibiotics. Chronic ear problems don't happen just because airflow to the ear canal is inhibited by your Blue Lacy's medium and triangular ears. Frequently, they're a byproduct of other health problems, like allergies and yeast overgrowth. Pesticides, in the form of flea and tick control products or residue on food ingredients, have been blamed for chronic ear problems, as have vaccinations. If your Blue Lacy suffers from one ear infection after another, and antibiotics and steroidal ointments aren't addressing the cause, consider seeking advice from a holistic veterinarian. This way you can try to find the source of the problem, rather than just addressing the symptoms.

Ear Cleaning

If your Blue Lacy 's ears have a lot of brown, waxy discharge, you may need to clean them to keep him comfortable. You can buy a lot of veterinary preparations for cleaning out the ear, but an easier method is simply to warm

Chapter Seven: Vet Care for Your Blue Lacy

some olive oil, dip a cotton ball in it, and gently wipe the underside of your Blue Lacy's ear flap.

Don't become a zealot about keeping your Blue Lacy's ears clean and plucked. In a healthy dog, frequent cleaning should not be necessary. Putting too much liquid in the ear can cause ear problems, and plucking the hair in the ear canal can irritate it. If your Blue Lacy 's ears look good and smell sweet, don't rock the boat by cleaning and plucking.

Lameness or Limping

An active dog can get an occasional limp that's nothing to worry about. He might have something as simple as a pulled muscle, an abrasion on his paw, or a charley horse. However, if it goes on for a while or the pain seems extreme, it might be something more serious.

Toe Problems

A torn toenail can cause your Blue Lacy to limp. If your dog tears a nail off, apply pressure with a cloth to stop the bleeding. If the nail isn't torn completely off, take him to the veterinarian, who can finish the job, sedating him if necessary.

Although a nail can be torn if your dog is playing hard in the grass, this damage can also be a sign of an autoimmune problem called lupoid onchodystrophy. If your Blue Lacy tears more than one nail, talk to your vet about the possibility of an underlying issue.

Chapter Seven: Vet Care for Your Blue Lacy

If a lump develops under your Blue Lacy's toenail, consult your vet. He might have toe cancer (squamous cell carcinoma, or SCC). More than one toe may be involved over a period of time. Treatment involves amputating the toe to stop spreading of the cancer.

Other Causes of Limping

Whether or not you can find an obvious cause for it, don't ignore a persistent limp. Not only is it an indication that your Blue Lacy is in pain, a chronic limp can also be a sign of a potentially serious problem. Particularly if he's older, a limp might indicate that your Blue Lacy has the beginning of degenerative joint disease (arthritis).

Probably the scariest source of a limp is bone cancer (osteosarcoma). A limp that shifts from leg to leg can be a sign of polyarthritis, an autoimmune condition. In addition, a limp might mean a strained or torn cruciate ligament, a condition that seems increasingly common in dogs. Surgery is usually required to repair the torn knee ligament.

If your dog is limping but is using the leg and doesn't seem to be in much pain, you can take a wait-and-see approach. Make a note of it in your calendar. If the limp goes away within a day or two, chalk it up to something minor. But if the limp persists, or your Blue Lacy is refusing to put weight on the leg, take him to the vet immediately.

Chapter Eight: Showing Your Blue Lacy

Showing your Blue Lacy in conformation shows may well cater to your inner competitive streak, but it also has a more important function than an individual dog simply getting placed and being in the line-up to receive a rosette. For a beginner, this may suffice as a first goal, but here's a glimpse of the bigger picture. Breeders continually try to produce dogs that match their breed standard as closely as possible. If a dog does not match the standard exactly possibly he has a wavy rather than a straight coat – this is called a fault, or a deviation from the breed standard. Breeders strive to eradicate that fault in their lines by a careful selection of dogs to breed from, although it may take many generations to remove the fault entirely. No dog, however, is ever a

Chapter Eight: Showing Your Blue Lacy

complete match to the standard, and all deviate from it to a greater or lesser degree.

How Do You Know If Your Dog Is Good Enough to Show?

The first time that you may have thought about showing perhaps came when the breeder suggested that the puppy you are buying might be a good prospect for the show ring, and asked if you would show him. The breeder's thoughts on an eight-week-old puppy, unfortunately, don't guarantee you success as the puppy may not go on to fulfil his potential. But such encouragement from the breeder is obviously a good start to your showing career.

Dogs which have success in the show ring don't always come from a breeder with experience of exhibiting. Pet bitches are often mated with Show Champion dogs and, while there is no knowing how well the bitch matches up to the breed standard, sometimes very good show dogs appear from pet homes. In these circumstances you don't have a knowledgeable breeder to guide you, so it's a matter of trying to interpret the breed standard and being as objective as possible when evaluating your puppy or dog against the criteria. Going to shows, looking at the dogs in the ring and mentally comparing your dog to others will also give you some pointers as to whether he could have any success. If you have knowledgeable friends, then you could ask them to look at him for you.

Chapter Eight: Showing Your Blue Lacy

Preparing to Show Your Dog

Whether you've just collected an eight-week-old puppy or have an adolescent or older dog, there's a lot of preparation to do before you even think of stepping inside a show ring. It's not just knowing what to do, it's being able to do it. The effort and training you put in from the time when you first collect your puppy will pay dividends in your showing career.

What Age Does My Dog Need to Be to Start to Show?

Most shows are licensed by the Kennel Club and run under their rules and regulations. Until your puppy is six months old you will not be able to exhibit him at most Kennel Club licensed events, but there is no upper age limit – dogs can start showing at any time in their lives. If you have a young puppy, that first show can seem a long way away, but there's a whole list of things you can do in the intervening time to prepare him, and you, for your first formal show. If you're considering showing an older dog, you'll both benefit from training before entering the show ring.

Socialization

Whether or not you end up showing your puppy, it is essential that you start to socialize him as soon as you bring him home. This means getting him used to as many sights and

Chapter Eight: Showing Your Blue Lacy

sounds as possible. The experiences he has during his first six- teen weeks of life will have a great influence on his character and behavior as an adult. A show dog, in particular, needs to be able to act appropriately around other dogs and strangers, including both adults and children. Shows are noisy and busy places. There will be the general hubbub caused by a large number of people chatting, tannoys announcing classes and people clapping the winners. There will be people, dogs, crates and trolleys being pushed past where you are standing. You'll find pushchairs, wheel-chairs, mobility scooters and people with walking sticks at shows, and your dog needs to be able to stay calm and untroubled while they are going by. Even before your puppy has completed his vaccinations, he can be carried out and about to expose him to new situations. Let different people stroke and fuss him. He will need to get used to judges going over him so he mustn't flinch away from strangers. Try to make sure he meets children of all ages, and people of all skin colors. Some people recommend taking him to somewhere like a car boot sale, where there will be a host of different activities going on, and where a cute puppy will attract attention from young and old alike. Some dogs are easier to socialize than others, and a naturally aloof breed might take a lot more effort to prepare them for the show ring. But the more you expose him to at a young age, the less scared and fearful he'll be of new things as an adult. You may consider taking your young puppy to a show just for the experience. Local fun shows, which are not run under Kennel Club rules, are generally less strict when it comes to puppies, and are good places to take him to familiarize him with the hustle and bustle of the show environment. He may even be able to enter a puppy class before he's six months old. Be

Chapter Eight: Showing Your Blue Lacy

careful that you don't overwhelm him though – his first experience should be positive and fun, as you don't want to put him off showing for life! Once your puppy is four months old you might, at the discretion of the society running the show, be able to take him to any Kennel Club licensed show as a 'Not for Competition' dog. This means that you will probably have to pay an entry fee to take your puppy in, but you will not be able to compete.

If it's a benched show, he will usually be allocated a bench. The benefit is clearly that the experience will be good for both you and your puppy. If the schedule doesn't make it clear whether you can take him or not, you may need to contact the secretary organizing the show to check whether they allow young puppies to at- tend. Under the terms of their insurance, Kennel Club licensed shows cannot permit dogs or puppies to be present at shows without being disclosed in advance on the entry form.

Ringcraft

Although you can read books and magazines, look up articles on the internet or watch YouTube videos, there is no substitute for going to a good ringcraft training class to find out what goes on in the show ring and how to present your dog in the best possible way. From as early an age as possible you should start to stand or stack your dog, and, if it applies to your breed, get him accustomed to standing on a table. He needs to get used to someone he doesn't know approaching him, looking in his mouth at his teeth and

Chapter Eight: Showing Your Blue Lacy

running their hands all over his body and, in the case of a dog, to check whether he has both testicles descended. You'll get the help you need to do this at your local ringcraft class; these provide specific training for show dogs and handlers. It's useful to contact the society or club as soon as you know you're getting a puppy so that you can enroll him and be ready to start attending classes as soon as his course of vaccinations has been completed and he is able to go out and mix with other dogs.

Training for the Show Ring

You cannot just rely on weekly training classes to prepare your dog for the show ring; you will also need to put in a lot of practice at home. Training your new puppy for the show ring might well have already begun by the time you collect him if you are buying from a breeder who specifically breeds pups to show. Often breeders will have started getting the pups used to being handled, and teaching them to stand. How much training has been done will depend partly on the size of the litter – a breeder with a small litter will have far more time to devote to each, than one with a litter of fourteen or more! Whether or not any pre-training has been done, if you are going to show your new puppy, it's never too early to start. The essentials are that your puppy will need to stand still and be able to concentrate on you while ignoring distractions.

Chapter Eight: Showing Your Blue Lacy

Using bait

Bait is the word used in showing to describe the treats or titbits used in the show ring either to reward the dog for good behavior, or to get his attention. In some breeds bait is thrown in the air to make the dog look up. Bait is a two-edged sword. It is useful for training, but some dogs become so fixated on the reward that they can think of nothing else, and don't offer the behavior that they should be being rewarded for. If bait is used to try to make a dog move nicely beside the handler, there is the risk that, instead of moving nicely, he will run and constantly jump up to get the treat. Likewise, a dog taught to stand by chewing at a piece of bait may not want to stop nibbling and open his mouth for the judge to inspect his teeth. Most people start by using bait in training, but it's good to be aware that as behavior is learned, rewards should start to become physical (i.e. fusses, stroking), rather than edible. You can still reward him with a treat, but less often. It will make life much easier in the ring if the dog expects a reward on exit from the ring, not all the time he is being judged. Throwing food around in the ring or using squeaky toys to get a dog's attention are activities which are not welcomed by other exhibitors. Whatever you choose to train with initially, work towards getting your dog's attention or rewarding him for the right behavior without the use of any support items. Your life will be easier, and your fellow exhibitors will thank you for it.

Starting to stand your dog

Chapter Eight: Showing Your Blue Lacy

Smaller dogs are placed on a table for judging, and this is a useful place to start with all puppies when they are little. Training sessions should be short as a young puppy has a very short attention span. Begin by getting your puppy to stand still for a few seconds, and then reward him with lots of fuss. A popular method of persuading a wriggly puppy to stand still is to use a tube of soft cheese as bait. This treat doesn't run out, and he can lick away while you are placing his feet. Say 'Stand' or whatever word you are going to use so he associates the action with the command. Practicing a few times every day for a short time is far better than lengthy training sessions.

What to take

It is useful to keep a bag packed with the essentials so you don't need to rush around finding everything early on the show day. Suggested items are:

- Show lead
- Ring clip or armband to hold your ring number. (Ring clips can range from
- plain and simple to special ones for your breed. If you choose an armband make sure it's not loose so that it will slip down your arm as you move. You can find clips online or purchase them at some shows.)
- Treats or bait if you use them in the ring
- Slobber cloth (if you have a breed likely to drool)
- Grooming kit and wet wipes

Chapter Eight: Showing Your Blue Lacy

- Poo bags (always keep one handy in your pocket in case of accidents in
- the ring)
- Schedule and map
- Proof of entry
- Water and water bowl for your dog
- Blanket and benching chain for benched shows
- Crate, cage or carrying box if you are using one, plus identification label
- Trolley (if you have a lot to carry)
- Dog toy (to keep him amused but not a squeaky one as it may annoy other
- exhibitors)
- Wet weather gear for you and your dog (essential if the venue is outdoors,
- but don't forget you may have a long way to walk from the car park to the show venue even if it is being held indoors)
- Umbrella for shade on hot days
- Copy of your dog's pedigree (in case someone asks)
- Refreshments for you (normally there will be somewhere to buy food and
- drink, though it may be expensive)

Chapter Eight: Showing Your Blue Lacy

Chapter Nine: Breeding Your Blue Lacy

Breeding dogs is not something that you should do on a whim and certainly not something you should do for money. If you think that breeding your dog will be a good way to make a little extra cash you are probably wrong. You will be lucky to come out even, by the time you cover expenses to care for a pregnant female and a litter of puppies. You should only breed your Blue Lacy if you thoroughly prepare yourself through in-depth research. You also need to be sure that you are able to provide the level of care required. You will learn the basics about breeding Blue Lacys in this chapter.

Chapter Nine: Breeding Your Blue Lacy

Basic Breeding Information

I am all in favor of breeding at least one litter of pups in order to keep the generation going of your beloved pet. If you do not wish to breed with your dog, or only intend to breed one litter, you may wish to consider the benefits to your dog's health of spaying or neutering.

There is much debate about when is the ideal time to spay or neuter a dog. Traditionally between 6 months and a year was considered ideal. According to 'Blue Cross' they advocate spaying or neutering before the age of 6 months, but for larger dogs this should be after the first heat. However, according to the ASPCA, they suggest dogs can be spayed before 6 months of age. Spaying a female dog before her first heat is considered to significantly reduce your dog's risk for developing mammary cancer as well as ovarian and uterine cancers.

If you are considering the option of breeding your Blue Lacy, you will find it useful to know some facts about dog breeding in general. For example, the oestrus cycle (also known as "heat") for dogs occurs twice a year; about every 6 months; though some small-breed dogs have three cycles per year. This cycle typically lasts for 14 to 21 days with the length varying from one dog to another. It can take a few years for an adult dog's cycle to become regular. Heat does not occur in any particular season; it is simply a matter of the dog's age and when she reaches breeding age.

If you plan to breed your Blue Lacy, it will be important for you to recognize the signs of oestrus. The first sign that your dog is going into heat will be the swelling of the external

Chapter Nine: Breeding Your Blue Lacy

vulva. In some cases, your dog may excrete a bloody discharge early on but this typically does not develop until the 5th to 7th day of the cycle. As your dog's cycle progresses, the discharge will become lighter in colour and more watery. By the 10th day of her cycle, the discharge will be pinkish in colour.

In addition to swelling of the vulva and a bloody discharge, many female Blue Lacys in heat will start to urinate more often than usual. You may also notice an increased appetite. Sometimes the dog will develop marking behaviour, spraying urine on various objects in the home to mark her territory and to attract male dogs. A male dog can smell a female in heat from great distances, so it is very important that you keep your female Blue Lacy indoors when she is in heat. When you take her outside, supervise her closely and never take her to a dog park or anywhere that intact male dogs may be present.

Ovulation typically occurs at the time of your dog's cycle when the vaginal discharge becomes watery. During ovulation is when your Blue Lacy will be most fertile. If you intend to breed her, this is when you should introduce her to the male dog. Your Blue Lacy may not be receptive to the advances of a male dog until this point in her cycle. However, she is capable of becoming pregnant at any point during oestrus because sperm can survive for up to 5 days in the female's reproductive tract. If your female Blue Lacy accidentally mates with the wrong dog you can take her to the veterinarian for a mis-mating injection. Be aware, however, that there are risks associated with this injection, so discuss it carefully with your vet.

Chapter Nine: Breeding Your Blue Lacy

The number of puppies your Blue Lacy carries may vary. The average litter size is about 6 puppies, but up to 10 is not unusual and for a first litter there may only be 1 or 2. In most cases, new mothers will have smaller litters at first and then may carry more puppies until about her fourth litter when the number tapers off again.

Once your Blue Lacy becomes pregnant, she will enter into a gestation period lasting about 63 days (9 weeks). You will not be able to detect your dog's pregnancy until the pregnancy has advanced about 3 weeks. Do not attempt to feel for the foetuses on your own because you could hurt your dog or the developing foetuses. An experienced veterinarian will be able to palpate your dog's uterus around day 28 to 32 of her pregnancy to confirm that she is indeed pregnant. It is safe to perform an ultrasound on a pregnant dog after 25 days, and by six weeks, pregnancy can be confirmed using x-rays.

The Breeding Process

Again, it is debatable as to the best age for a dogs first litter. It is generally considered to breed after the first or second season. The bitch should by this point be fully sexually mature You will start to recognize the signs of heat in your dog and will be able to take precautions against accidental pregnancies. An intact male dog can smell a female in heat from distances up to 3 miles (4.83 km). So do not think that just because your neighbours do not have a dog that your female will be safe. The whole season process takes

Chapter Nine: Breeding Your Blue Lacy

approximately 3 weeks until your female is safe. Usually by the 18th day of oestrus, the female is still likely to attract the attention of males, but she is unlikely to 'stand' for them. In this respect, she should be safe from any unwanted pregnancies.

Once your dogs are of proper breeding age, you can start to think about breeding. You will need to keep a record of your female dog's oestrus cycle so you will know when she is most fertile; around days 11 to 15 of the cycle. During this time is when your female dog will be most receptive to breeding. So, that is when you should introduce her to the male dog. Mating behavior usually involves the male dog mounting the female from behind. The male will ejaculate his sperm into the female's reproductive tract where it will fertilize the eggs. Sometimes the two dogs become what is known as 'tied'. Effectively the male is unable to release his penis from the female vagina. So do not become distressed or try to release him in anyway. This is a perfectly natural occurrence and he will release himself in a short length of time. If the eggs are fertilized, conception occurs and the female becomes pregnant. She then enters into the gestation period which, as previously noted, lasts about 59 to 63 days.

It is also important to remember the health of the bitch prior to breeding. Obviously never consider mating her if she has some illness at the time. Even if it is a temporary skin disease that she could pass onto the pups. Ensure that any disease is clear before you breed. You should also ensure that

Chapter Nine: Breeding Your Blue Lacy

she is neither overweight, nor underweight. Obviously, you will restrict her diet if she looks too fat and feed her up if too thin.

The stud dog

The choice of a stud dog will depend on your intentions for breeding in the first place. If you are merely wishing to keep the lineage of your beloved pet, you will no doubt choose a healthy dog with a good pedigree. If you are much more serious about showing, then the pedigree and therefore stud dog, will be very specific towards a dog with a top show pedigree. You can always check with the KC or AKC for their recommendation of top breeders. Once you find a suitable stud dog, it is likely that you will have to arrange to travel to or board your dog with them in order to facilitate a successful mating. This is obviously something you need to plan, so keeping records of the oestrus cycle and therefore the optimum time to mate, is vital.

Stages of Pregnancy

Again, you must keep track of when you breed your female dog so you will know when to expect her to whelp the puppies (give birth). Once again, by the third week of pregnancy, around day 21, your veterinarian will be able to confirm whether the dog is pregnant or not. He may also be able to give you an estimate as to her litter size. Treat your

Chapter Nine: Breeding Your Blue Lacy

pregnant female as you normally would until the fourth or fifth week of pregnancy, then you should start to increase her feeding rations proportionally with her weight gain. You only need to increase your dog's diet slightly to account for her increased nutritional needs. Having said that, your dog will know how much she needs to eat, so you may be able to let her feed freely rather than rationing her food. Her feed intake is giving nutrition to her growing pups as well as herself. So, in this respect, you do not need to worry about any overfeeding leading to obesity, and you certainly do not want to underfeed her. Your pregnant dog's diet should be high in protein and animal fat with plenty of calcium.

It is also around this time that your Blue Lacy will start to look visibly pregnant. Your dog's belly will grow larger, tighter, and harder and her nipples will become especially swollen during the last week of pregnancy.

Maintaining everyday care

During her pregnancy you should carry on her normal routine of regular feeds and exercise. As she gets heavier, she is unlikely to be inclined to race about as normal. However, you should ensure that she is not placed into any excitable situations, which may cause her to chase after something, or play energetically with another dog. But you should make sure that she does still have daily moderate exercise. It is also a good idea to keep up with grooming her. If she has a

Chapter Nine: Breeding Your Blue Lacy

noticeable discharge from the vulva, then it is important that you wash the area on a daily basis, with warm water. This will of course keep the area clean, but also avoid discharge deposits around the house.

It is also a good idea to weigh the mother once per week on the same day, to keep an accurate record. You will no doubt notice her getting bigger anyway, but weighing her confirms that the pregnancy and pup growth is normal. At approximately the fifth to sixth week of pregnancy, you should notice her breast get firmer.

Raising Blue Lacy Puppies

Whelping box

By the eighth week of your dog's pregnancy, in other words approximately a week before she gives birth, you will need to provide her with a whelping box. You can easily and cheaply construct a whelping box out of ply board with either metal brackets to hold the box together or four pieces of 2 inch by 2-inch timber for each corner. The height of the box should be about 15 inches high, with a front cutaway section about 10 inches high to allow the bitch easy access, but ensuring that pups cannot easily crawl out of the box. If you are not DIY inclined, you can buy relatively cheap cardboard disposable boxes. Simply do a Google search for [whelping box], and you will be presented with a number of possibilities. Whatever box you use, it should be a comfortable place lined with clean, old blankets and towels where she can give birth and care for the puppies. Remember that you may need to change the

Chapter Nine: Breeding Your Blue Lacy

bedding from time to time if it becomes soiled, so have spare replacement blankets/towels to hand. It is best to place this box in a quiet area where your dog will not be disturbed. If you put it somewhere that is too bright or noisy, she will just find somewhere else to whelp. She should be allowed to spend time in the box and therefore accept this as the best place to give birth. You should also make sure this room is warm and draft free.

Whelping: Other supplies

Ideally, as well as the whelping box, you should prepare yourself with important supplies to have on hand when the time comes. Hopefully you have a spare room or at the very least a corner set up especially as a nursery. I would recommend getting hold of a large cardboard box to place the various items that you may need. The following list will equip you with essential supplies for the whelping as follows:

- A heat source; this can be a heat lamp, heat pad etc. (as an emergency provision hot water bottles have been known to come in very handy) This is of course to keep the mother and pups warm.
- Clean towels intended to clean up anything the mother does not.
- A couple of rolls of paper toweling will also be handy as an extra back up for cleaning.

Chapter Nine: Breeding Your Blue Lacy

- Newspapers will be handy if you need to change the floor covering which could get wet.

- If you have to cut the umbilical cord, a pair of blunt end scissors, surgical or white thread to tie off the end, cotton wool and antiseptic solution to dab an open wound and clean it. It will be a good idea to have a separate, sterile container to put these items in, to minimize infection. A container with surgical spirit/antiseptic solution, is also a good idea to keep items such as the scissors or a rectal thermometer to check temperatures.

- You may also wish to weigh the puppies, so a pair of suitable scales will be necessary.

Final stages of pregnancy and giving birth

During the last week of your Blue Lacy's pregnancy you should start checking her internal temperature regularly. Using a rectal thermometer, the normal body temperature for a dog should read between 100°F and 102°F (37.7°C to 38.8°C). However, your female dog's body temperature will drop about 24 hours before contractions begin. Your dog's body temperature may drop as low as 98°F (36.6°C), so when you notice a drop in your dog's temperature you can be sure that it won't be long before the puppies arrive. Your dog will also start spending more time in the whelping box at this time. You can check on her occasionally, but do not disturb her too much or she might go elsewhere to whelp. There are other signs that her giving birth is imminent, these include; general restlessness, making nests, moving blankets about or tearing

Chapter Nine: Breeding Your Blue Lacy

up paper you may have lying around, she may refuse food etc. It may be nothing immediately to worry about, but you can be sure she will soon go into labor.

If she goes into labor during the day, if you can, stay with her as much as possible. This is particularly important if this is her first pregnancy, as she may be anxious and need your reassurance.

When your Blue Lacy goes into labor, you will notice obvious signs of discomfort. She may start pacing restlessly and panting, switching from one position to another without seeming to get comfortable. The early stages of labor can last for several hours with contractions occurring about 10 minutes apart. This usually occurs in waves of 3 to 5 contractions followed by a period of rest. If your Blue Lacy has two hours of contractions without any puppies being born, take her to the vet immediately. Without a veterinary diagnosis, it is difficult to ascertain what the problem may be, but as with human pregnancies, she may need a caesarean section.

Once your Blue Lacy starts whelping, the puppies will generally arrive every thirty minutes; following ten to thirty minutes of forceful straining from the female.

When a puppy is born, the mother will clean the puppy and bite off the umbilical cord. Not only does the licking, clean the puppy, but it helps to stimulate its breathing as well. You need to let the mother do this without you attempting to handle the puppies unless something goes wrong. If this does not happen use a clean towel to clean the puppy and make sure there is no membrane covering the puppies' muzzle.

Chapter Nine: Breeding Your Blue Lacy

Sometimes the mother may appear to be struggling to give birth to one of the pups. Its head or its back legs may be stuck out and not going anywhere. It may be necessary for you to help her by wrapping a clean towel around the pup and gently pulling. CAUTION: Only pull when the mother is obviously pushing. Some people advise against helping the mother in this way. But if you get a pup that is being delivered legs first, there is a possibility that the umbilical cord could be wrapped around the pup and potentially strangling it.

If a puppy is not breathing

If the puppy appears to not be breathing, you will need to administer emergency first aid. Wrap the pup in a clean towel and hold his body firmly, upside down in the palms of your hand, as if you were praying, his head should be facing the ground. Now shake him back and forth but not too vigorously, in an attempt to stimulate him into action. If he fails to breath, rub his ribs. Next attempt the Heimlich manoesuvre as follows: Again, turn the pup upside down, holding him with his back pressed to your chest. Clasp your hands on his abdomen, just below the ribs. Now give 5 thrusts, reasonably hard and sharp to the abdomen. Now look inside the mouth or if there is some mucous or object expelled, if so, remove this.

If you still have no luck, artificial respiration will probably be your last resort. In this case, it is similar to CPR that you would administer to a human and the following would be the same for an adult dog. You will need to blow air into the pup's nose and mouth. Some people prefer to use a plastic food bag

Chapter Nine: Breeding Your Blue Lacy

with one corner cut off that you place over the pup's nose/mouth, so that you are not getting his full muzzle/hair etc. in your mouth.

The procedure should be as follows:

1. Lay the pup on his right side

2. Place your hand or fingers on his ribs at the point the elbow meets the chest/ribs (this is approximately where his heart is). Some breeders will simply hold the pup firmly and simply compress the ribs. Be very careful doing this, as although this is an emergency, you do not want to break the rib cage.

3. Give about 20 compressions per minute. You do this in short bursts. So, 60 divided by 20 gives is 3.

4. You should be able to check his pulse in the place where the elbow meets the chest or around his wrist above his front paw.

5. Repeat once more, and if there is still no pulse/breathing, give mouth to mouth resuscitation.

6. So as above, either place a plastic bag with the corner removed over the pup's mouth or simply cup your own mouth over the pup's nose and mouth (You should make sure that you make a seal so that no air escapes, and gently blow but similar to how you would breathe out after taking a deep breath. You should now give 3 compressions and then breath air into the pup.

Chapter Nine: Breeding Your Blue Lacy

7. Continue this sequence until hopefully the pup starts to breathe. Don't just give up after a few minutes, at least continue until an emergency vet arrives.

Hopefully you will never have to experience this, but it is best to be aware of what to do just in case.

After the mother has given birth

After all of the puppies have been whelped, again the female will expel the rest of the placenta and then allow the puppies to nurse (feed). The bitch may attempt to eat the placenta, which is normal. It is advisable at this stage to get a veterinary check up to confirm that the bitch is healthy and to confirm all of the placentas have been expelled and not likely to cause an internal infection.

It is very important that the puppies start nursing (feeding) within 1 hour of delivery because this is when they will get the colostrum. If there is obviously a pup that has not made its way to the mother's breast soon after it is born then place it on a teat or close by. The colostrum is the first milk produced by the mother and it is loaded not only with vitamins and minerals. It also contains antibodies that will protect the puppies against illness and infection while their own immune systems are developing. After whelping, your female dog will be very hungry, so give her as much food as she will eat. As previously said, do not be alarmed if she consumes the expelled placenta as well. Please remember to count the placenta, as it is possible one or two could remain in the mother and cause an infection if not expelled. In this case she would need veterinary attention. Again, do not just

Chapter Nine: Breeding Your Blue Lacy

leave the placentas left, and if it is practical to do so, remove any remaining along with soiled newspapers.

Blue Lacy puppies are born with their eyes and ears closed. They will also have very little fur, so they are completely dependent on their mother for warmth and care. If you suspect that the pups are not warm enough or are likely to chill over-night, consider getting hold of a heat lamp. This can be sighted above the whelping area. Care must be taken not to overheat either them or the mother. So, it is perhaps best to place this at one end or a corner, therefore leaving a part of the whelping area cooler.

Growing puppies

The puppies will spend most of their day nursing and sleeping until their eyes start to open around 3 weeks of age. Between the third and sixth week after birth is when the puppies will start to become more active, playing with each other and exploring the whelping box area. The puppies will also start to grow very quickly as long as you feed the mother enough so she can produce enough milk.

Around six weeks after birth is when you should start weaning the puppies if the mother has not started already. Start to offer the puppies small amounts of puppy food soaked in water or broth to soften it. The puppies may sample a bit of the food even as they are still nursing. But they should be fully transitioned onto solid food by eight weeks of age. If you do not plan to keep the puppies yourself, it is at this time that you should start introducing the puppies to potential buyers. You should never sell a puppy that has not been fully

Chapter Nine: Breeding Your Blue Lacy

weaned and you should carefully vet potential buyers to make sure that the puppies go to a good home.

Puppies are very impressionable during the first few months of life so you need to make sure they get as many experiences (socialization) as possible. If your puppies are not exposed to new things at a young age they will grow up to be fearful and nervous adults. Give the puppies plenty of toys to play with as their teeth start to grow in around week ten, and start playing with them yourself so they get used to being handled by humans.

Conclusion

You will need to remember the responsibility that a Blue Lacy brings. They need to be taught commands, taught what they're allowed to chew on and what they're not, taught where to pee and when. Everything that a dog needs to know, you are going to be teaching your puppy. This takes time and energy, but it will be a rewarding process in the end. Remember that adolescent Blue Lacy dogs are going to be more frustrating to deal with, but this is only a short stage your puppy goes through before becoming an adult. We covered training and discipline in chapter five, so that you know how to train yours properly, and when to expect the most difficulty.

We covered health and grooming in chapters six and seven. While grooming is mostly done for aesthetic and hygienic reasons, it can and should also be considered a part of keeping your Blue Lacy healthy. There are a lot of different ailments that you've read about in chapter seven, and can now keep an eye out for. One of the easiest ways to do this is to take the required time to groom your Blue Lacy. The short time you spend doing this will let you keep their coat in perfect condition, reduce the likelihood of illness due to dirt and grime, plus it will help you check for signs of health issues as well as bonding with your dog. So long as you practice the advice in these chapters, you will be able to keep your Blue Lacy in good shape while getting an early jump on any medical issues that crop up along the way.

It is my deepest hope that you bring a Blue Lacy into your family and see the joy and happiness they can bring into

Conclusion

your lives. Just make sure that you have considered all these needs and are able to provide them for your dog. They are family, after all, and so they should be treated as such. But I know you'll do exactly that.

Thank you for reading!

Glossary of Dog Terms

Adoption – A process in which a rescued pet is placed into a permanent home.

Acute Disease – refers to a disease or illness that manifests quickly

Agility – This is a sport in which the dog handler guides and instructs the dog through a course of obstacles while being timed. Accuracy through this obstacle course is paramount. The dogs must complete the obstacle course without a leash or toys (or food) as incentives. The handler can only use voice, movement and various body signals in order to direct the dog.

AKC – American Kennel Club, the largest purebred dog registry in the United States

Almond Eye – Referring to an elongated eye shape rather than a rounded shape

Apple Head – A round-shaped skull

Balance – A show term referring to all of the parts of the dog, both moving and standing, which produce a harmonious image

Beard – Long, thick hair on the dog's underjaw

Best in Show – An award given to the only undefeated dog left standing at the end of judging

Bitch – A female dog

Bite – The position of the upper and lower teeth when the dog's jaws are closed; positions include level, undershot, scissors, or overshot

Blaze – A white stripe running down the center of the face between the eyes

Board – To house, feed, and care for a dog for a fee

Breed – A domestic race of dogs having a common gene pool and characterized appearance/function

Breed Standard – A published document describing the look, movement, and behavior of the perfect specimen of a particular breed

Buff – An off-white to gold coloring

Canine- a term for dog.

Canine Teeth- also known as eye teeth, the largest teeth found in the dog's mouth. They are long, curved teeth on either side of the mouth, top and bottom.

Chronic Disease – refers to a disease that will last indefinitely.

Clip – A method of trimming the coat in some breeds

Coat – The hair covering of a dog; some breeds have two coats, and outer coat and undercoat; also known as a double coat. Examples of breeds with double coats include German Shepherd, Siberian Husky, Akita, etc.

Condition – The health of the dog as shown by its skin, coat, behavior, and general appearance

Crate – A container used to house and transport dogs; also called a cage or kennel

Crossbreed (Hybrid) – A dog having a sire and dam of two different breeds; cannot be registered with the AKC

Dam (bitch) – The female parent of a dog;

Dock – To shorten the tail of a dog by surgically removing the end part of the tail.

Double Coat – Having an outer weather-resistant coat and a soft, waterproof coat for warmth; see above.

Drop Ear – An ear in which the tip of the ear folds over and hangs down; not prick or erect

Entropion – A genetic disorder resulting in the upper or lower eyelid turning in

Fancier – A person who is especially interested in a particular breed or dog sport

Fawn – A red-yellow hue of brown

Feathering – A long fringe of hair on the ears, tail, legs, or body of a dog

Groom – To brush, trim, comb or otherwise make a dog's coat neat in appearance

Heel – To command a dog to stay close by its owner's side

Hip Dysplasia – A condition characterized by the abnormal formation of the hip joint

Inbreeding – The breeding of two closely related dogs of one breed

Kennel – A building or enclosure where dogs are kept

Litter – A group of puppies born at one time

Markings – A contrasting color or pattern on a dog's coat

Mask – Dark shading on the dog's foreface

Mate – To breed a dog and a bitch

Neuter – To castrate a male dog or spay a female dog

Pads – The tough, shock-absorbent skin on the bottom of a dog's foot

Parti-Color – A coloration of a dog's coat consisting of two or more definite, well-broken colors; one of the colors must be white

Pedigree – The written record of a dog's genealogy going back three generations or more

Pied – A coloration on a dog consisting of patches of white and another color

Prick Ear – Ear that is carried erect, usually pointed at the tip of the ear

Puppy – A dog under 12 months of age

Purebred – A dog whose sire and dam belong to the same breed and who are of unmixed descent

Saddle – Colored markings in the shape of a saddle over the back; colors may vary

Shedding – The natural process whereby old hair falls off the dog's body as it is replaced by new hair growth.

Sire – The male parent of a dog

Smooth Coat – Short hair that is close-lying

Spay – The surgery to remove a female dog's ovaries, rendering her incapable of breeding

Trim – To groom a dog's coat by plucking or clipping

Undercoat – The soft, short coat typically concealed by a longer outer coat

Vaccine – a shot that is given to a dog to help produce immunity to a specific disease.

Wean – The process through which puppies transition from subsisting on their mother's milk to eating solid food

Whelping – The act of birthing a litter of puppies

Index

A

accidents	78
adoption	8
age	37, 126, 137
allergies	36, 102
appearance	140
appetite	12, 109
attention	49, 64
award	139

B

baby gates	15
bait	119
barking	65
bedding	15
behavior	62
bitch	142
biting	68
body	142
breathing	133
breeder	114
breeding	122

C

cage	140
canine	5, 93
care	99
castrate	142
checklist	16
chewing	69

clicker	23, 55
coat	6, 91, 142
collar	24
coloration	142
colors	142
comb	141
come	52
command	54, 141
commands	45
condition	141
crate	14
crate training	79

D

dam	141, 142
diarrhea	35, 107
disorder	141
dog park	80
door	73
double coat	140
drink	16

E

ear	96
eat	16
eating	143
energetic	6
equipment	13
exercise	48, 69
eyes	37

F

face	140
feeding	32
female	123, 135, 139, 143
food	17, 32
foot	142
foxtails	105

G

gene	140
genealogy	142
genetic	141
grooming	20, 88
growth	142
guard dogs	6

H

hair	90, 142
harness	24, 81
health	12
heel	59
herding dog	6
hip	141
home	14, 25
house	140
human food	38

I

intelligent	6

J

jumping 72

K

kibble 33

L

labor 132
lay down 47
leash 24, 81
leave 54
limp 111
litter 143
lumps 106

M

maintenance 6
male 124
markings 142
meal 34
milk 143
mites 90

N

nail clippers 95
nails 21, 95
neutering 123

O

obedience training	86
outer coat	143
Owning	13

P

parasites	90
parent	141
poop	77
position	49
pregnancy	125
puppies	143
purebred	10

R

record	142
rescues	9
reward	58
ringcraft	117
routine	76, 92

S

scrapes	105
shake	57
shampoo	20
sheddings	6
shelter	8
show ring	115
signal	51
sire	141, 142
sit	46

skills 59
skin 91, 142
social 72
spay 142
spaying 123
spray 19
stand 120
stay 49
stud 127
supplements 37
supplies 14, 130
surgery 143

T

tail 141
teeth 18, 67, 97, 140
temperament 6
temperature 83, 100
toilet training 74
tools 13
toothbrush 22
touch 56
toxic 38
toys 24, 71
treats 18, 22, 84
trimming 140

U

undercoat 140

V

veterinarian 101

vitamins 17
vomiting 107

W

wait 51
walk 60
water 36, 93
weight 37
whelping 129

Photo Credits

Page 3, mrod via Canva.com (Canva Pro License)

https://www.canva.com/photos/MAEEjfD1NXc-blue-lacy/

Page 7, TrueBlueLacys via Wikimedia Commons

https://commons.m.wikimedia.org/wiki/File:Blue_Lacy_3.jpg

Page 13, Firn via Canva.com (Canva Pro License)

https://www.canva.com/photos/MAEE7asyhnM-flat-lay-of-various-dog-supplies-for-training-or-travelling-on-gray-background/

Page 32, izzzy71 via Canva.com (Canva Pro License)

https://www.canva.com/photos/MADaAlhkZnM-dog-food-in-the-bowl-and-bone-shaped-biscuits/

Page 45, Wavetop via Canva.com (Canva Pro License)

https://www.canva.com/photos/MADerx9V8cY-dog-training-banner/

Page 88, Anna-av via Canva.com (Canva Pro License)

https://www.canva.com/photos/MADargh3NM8-trimming-claws-manicure-and-pedicure-grooming/

Page 99, Sakan Piriyapongsak via Canva.com (Canva Pro License)

https://www.canva.com/photos/MADatVQP3dY-veterinarian-or-student-wear-latex-gloves-using-syringe-an-injection-to-leg-white-dog-education-health-care-concept/

Page 113, Apple Tree House via Canva.com (Canva Pro License)

https://www.canva.com/photos/MAC7-T9e0Tg-three-small-dogs-with-winner-s-ribbons/

Page 122, Rainbowbrooke via Wikimedia Commons

https://commons.m.wikimedia.org/wiki/File:Blue_Lacy_Game_Dog.jpg

References

Blue Lacy- Dogtime.com

https://dogtime.com/dog-breeds/blue-lacy

Blue Lacy- Dogzone.com

https://www.dogzone.com/breeds/blue-lacy/

Blue Lacy: Dog Breed Profile- Thesprucepets.com

https://www.thesprucepets.com/blue-lacy-breed-profile-4769790

Blue Lacy- Dogbreedinfo.com

https://www.dogbreedinfo.com/bluelacy.htm

Blue Lacy- Nationalkennelclub.com

http://www.nationalkennelclub.com/breed-standards/blue-lacy.htm

Lacy Dog- Vetstreet.com

http://www.vetstreet.com/dogs/lacy-dog

Blue Lacy- 101dogbreeds.com

https://www.101dogbreeds.com/blue-lacy.asp

Blue Lacy- Dogsaholic.com

https://dogsaholic.com/breeds/profiles/blue-lacy.html

Blue Lacy- Dogbreedplus.com

https://www.dogbreedplus.com/dog_breeds/blue_lacy.php

Blue Lacy Dog Breed Information Center- Thehappypuppysite.com

https://thehappypuppysite.com/blue-lacy/

Blue Lacy- Globaldogbreeds.com

http://globaldogbreeds.com/Blue-Lacy.html

Things To know When Caring For Blue Lacys- Animalcaretip.com

https://animalcaretip.com/things-to-know-when-caring-for-blue-lacys/

Training a Blue Lacy Puppy- Petnedid.com

https://petnetid.com/breed/blue-lacy/training-a-blue-lacy-puppy/

Blue Lacy Dog- Dogsnet.com

https://dogsnet.com/blue-lacy-dog/

Blue Lacy- Dogsaholic.com

https://dogsaholic.com/breeds/profiles/blue-lacy.html

Blue Lacy- Dogmal.com

https://www.dogmal.com/blue-lacy/

Blue Lacy - Ruffchamp.com

https://ruffchamp.com/dog-breeds/blue-lacy-2-2/

Blue Lacy- Lacygamedog.com

http://www.lacygamedog.com/herd.html

Blue Lacy Dog Breed Information Guide- Barkpost.com

https://barkpost.com/answers/blue-lacy-dog-breed-information-guide/

Blue Lacy Dog- Roysfarm.com

https://www.roysfarm.com/blue-lacy-dog/

www.ingramcontent.com/pod-product-compliance
Lightning Source LLC
LaVergne TN
LVHW051834080426
835512LV00018B/2873